ROAN STALLION
TAMAR AND OTHER
POEMS

ROAN STALLION
TAMAR
and Other Poems

BY

ROBINSON JEFFERS

ROGUE
SCHOLAR

First published 1925

This edition © 2022
Rogue Scholar Press
All Rights Reserved

ISBN: 978-1-954357-09-9

To
UNA JEFFERS

Foreword

Robinson Jeffers is the greatest poet America has ever produced. It seems audacious to make that claim today when he has been all but forgotten, relegated to obscure university publications and environmentalist fan clubs. But there was a time when his visage graced the cover of *Time* magazine and his poetry was widely known and read—in another country, another America, now memory-holed like Jeffers himself. He is, as Jonathan Bowden said, the poet laureate of this other America, which once existed, if only in embryo, and which perhaps still exists in some form, outside of the media, outside of the cities, in the land and what remains of wild nature.

Jeffers' voice has a rare gravitas that one really only encounters in scripture and in the ancient classics. He is a man out of time, a man in whom eternal nature speaks to us, undiluted by the modern pathos because Jeffers has extricated himself from modernity. There on the California coast in the solitude of his rock tower at Tor House—which he built with his own hands—he composes his lines, and his charged words come down to us like Zarathustra from the mountains.

Jeffers is a Nietzschean, the rare sort who does not merely parrot and reformulate Nietzsche's ideas, but who, like Spengler or Ludwig Klages, learns from

Nietzsche *how to see*, and then goes on to apply this perception to wholly new sights and insights. As he wrote in 1938:

> Another formative principle came to me from a phrase of Nietzsche's: "The poets? The poets lie too much." I was nineteen when the phrase stuck in my mind; a dozen years passed before it worked effectively, and I decided not to tell lies in verse. Not to feign any emotion that I did not feel; not to pretend to believe in optimism or pessimism, or unreversible progress; not to say anything because it was popular, or generally accepted, or fashionable in intellectual circles, unless I myself believed it; and not to believe easily.

Jeffers shares with Nietzsche a deep commitment to truth at all costs—not the abstract Truth of philosophers and theologians but the raw truth of nature. For Jeffers is a nature poet, but not the quaint and tame nature of hippie romanticism, the abstracted and neutered nature that the urbanite goes to "experience" on weekends at a hiking trail or a tourist destination. Jeffers' nature is wild, undomesticated. It is Nietzsche's "monster of energy," overflowing with life, death, tragedy and beauty.

Jeffers sees humanity as insignificant, perhaps even as a mistake, but he does not see *life* this way. His philosophy of Inhumanism means to see the value of life not in humanity but outside of it, in nature. Some see in Jeffers a kind of Zen or Taoist sensibility, as in the poets of ancient China and Japan. But while Jeffers appreciates peace and tranquillity, he does not turn away from violence. His mysticism is based not on looking within, but without.

> Humanity is the start of the race; I say
> Humanity is the mold to break away from,
> the crust to break through,
> the coal to break into fire,
> The atom to be split.

He has an affinity with Hesiod, who also saw humans not as the center of creation but as a mere unfortunate appendage to it. When it comes to human affairs he shares the pessimism of the ancient Greeks like Heraclitus and Theognis, but he refuses to judge the natural world by human standards, with human values. This perhaps is part of what appealed to him in Nietzsche: to transvaluate all values not merely in order to create new *human* (all-too-human) values, but to transcend the human altogether to discover the eternal values of nature.

Jeffers is a Nietzschean but one can hardly call him a nihilist. In Jeffers' world there is not an absence of meaning but an overflowing of it. It is everywhere he looks, in the flight of the hawks and eagles, in the crashing of the waves on the rocks of the coast, in the passions and tragedies of human lives. It is only we who are alienated from nature who fail to find meaning, while Jeffers reminds us that nature is "divinely superfluous beauty."

It was with this volume which you now hold in your hands that Jeffers first burst onto the scene in 1925. It was reissued as a Modern Library edition in 1935, but has been sadly out of print for many years. We are proud to make it available once more and to introduce Robinson Jeffers to a new audience.

Rogue Scholar Press
Spring 2022

CONTENTS

ROAN STALLION

ROAN STALLION

The dog barked; then the woman stood in the doorway, and
    hearing iron strike stone down the steep road
Covered her head with a black shawl and entered the light
    rain; she stood at the turn of the road.
A nobly formed woman; erect and strong as a new tower;
    the features stolid and dark
But sculptured into a strong grace; straight nose with a high
    bridge, firm and wide eyes, full chin,
Red lips; she was only a fourth part Indian; a Scottish sailor
    had planted her in young native earth,
Spanish and Indian, twenty-one years before. He had named
    her California when she was born;
That was her name; and had gone north.
                              She heard the hooves and
    wheels come nearer, up the steep road.
The buckskin mare, leaning against the breastpiece, plodded
    into sight round the wet bank.
The pale face of the driver followed; the burnt-out eyes;
    they had fortune in them. He sat twisted
On the seat of the old buggy, leading a second horse by a
    long halter, a roan, a big one,
That stepped daintily; by the swell of the neck, a stallion.
    "What have you got, Johnny?" "Maskerel's stallion.
Mine now. I won him last night, I had very good luck."
    He was quite drunk. "They bring their mares up here
    now.
I keep this fellow. I got money besides, but I'll not show
    you." "Did you buy something, Johnny,
For our Christine? Christmas comes in two days, Johnny."
    "By God, forgot," he answered laughing.

"Don't tell Christine it's Christmas; after while I get her
    something, maybe."   But California:
"I shared your luck when you lost: you lost *me* once, Johnny,
    remember?   Tom Dell had me two nights
Here in the house: other times we've gone hungry: now
    that you've won, Christine will have her Christmas.
We share your luck, Johnny.   You give me money, I go down
    to Monterey to-morrow,
Buy presents for Christine, come back in the evening.   Next
    day Christmas."   "You have wet ride," he answered
Giggling.   "Here money.   Five dollar; ten; twelve dollar.
    You buy two bottles of rye whisky for Johnny."
"All right.   I go to-morrow."
                    He was an outcast Hollander; not old, but
    shriveled with bad living.
The child Christine inherited from his race blue eyes, from
    his life a wizened forehead; she watched
From the house-door her father lurch out of the buggy
    and lead with due respect the stallion
To the new corral, the strong one; leaving the wearily breath-
    ing buckskin mare to his wife to unharness.

Storm in the night; the rain on the thin shakes of the roof
    like the ocean on rock streamed battering; once thunder
Walked down the narrow canyon into Carmel valley and
    wore away westward; Christine was wakeful
With fears and wonders; her father lay too deep for storm
    to touch him.
                    Dawn comes late in the year's dark,
Later into the crack of a canyon under redwoods; and
    California slipped from bed
An hour before it; the buckskin would be tired; there was a
    little barley, and why should Johnny
Feed all the barley to his stallion?   That is what he would
    do.   She tiptoed out of the room.
Leaving her clothes, he'd waken if she waited to put them
    on, and passed from the door of the house

Into the dark of the rain; the big black drops were cold
  through the thin shift, but the wet earth
Pleasant under her naked feet.   There was a pleasant smell
  in the stable; and moving softly,
Touching things gently with the supple bend of the un-
  clothed body, was pleasant.   She found a box,
Filled it with sweet dry barley and took it down to the
  old corral.   The little mare sighed deeply
At the rail in the wet darkness; and California returning
  between two redwoods up to the house
Heard the happy jaws grinding the grain.   Johnny could
  mind the pigs and chickens.   Christine called to her
When she entered the house, but slept again under her hand.
  She laid the wet night-dress on a chair-back
And stole into the bedroom to get her clothes.   A plank
  creaked, and he wakened.   She stood motionless
Hearing him stir in the bed.   When he was quiet she stooped
  after her shoes, and he said softly,
"What are you doing?   Come back to bed."   "It's late, I'm
  going to Monterey, I must hitch up."
"You come to bed first.   I been away three days.   I give
  you money, I take back the money
And what you do in town then?"   She sighed sharply and
  came to the bed.
                  He reaching his hands from it
Felt the cool curve and firmness of her flank, and half rising
  caught her by the long wet hair.
She endured, and to hasten the act she feigned desire; she
  had not for long, except in dream, felt it.
Yesterday's drunkenness made him sluggish and exacting;
  she saw, turning her head sadly,
The windows were bright gray with dawn; he embraced her
  still, stopping to talk about the stallion.
At length she was permitted to put on her clothes.   Clear
  daylight over the steep hills;
Gray-shining cloud over the tops of the redwoods; the winter
  stream sang loud; the wheels of the buggy

Slipped in deep slime, ground on washed stones at the road-
    edge. Down the hill the wrinkled river smothered the
    ford.
You must keep to the bed of stones: she knew the way by
    willow and alder: the buckskin halted mid-stream,
Shuddering, the water her own color washing up to the traces;
    but California, drawing up
Her feet out of the whirl onto the seat of the buggy swung
    the whip over the yellow water
And drove to the road.
                    All morning the clouds were racing north-
    ward like a river. At noon they thickened.
When California faced the southwind home from Monterey
    it was heavy with level rainfall.
She looked seaward from the foot of the valley; red rays
    cried sunset from a trumpet of streaming
Cloud over Lobos, the southwest occident of the solstice.
    Twilight came soon, but the tired mare
Feared the road more than the whip. Mile after mile of slow
    gray twilight.
        Then, quite suddenly, darkness.
"Christine will be asleep. It is Christmas Eve. The ford.
    That hour of daylight wasted this morning!"
She could see nothing; she let the reins lie on the dashboard
    and knew at length by the cramp of the wheels
And the pitch down, they had reached it. Noise of wheels
    on stones, plashing of hooves in water; a world
Of sounds; no sight; the gentle thunder of water; the mare
    snorting, dipping her head, one knew,
To look for footing, in the blackness, under the stream. The
    hushing and creaking of the sea-wind
In the passion of invisible willows.
                    The mare stood still; the woman
    shouted to her; spared whip,
For a false leap would lose the track of the ford. She
    stood. "The baby's things," thought California,

"Under the seat: the water will come over the floor"; and
   rising in the midst of the water
She tilted the seat; fetched up the doll, the painted wooden
   chickens, the wooly bear, the book
Of many pictures, the box of sweets: she brought them all
   from under the seat and stored them, trembling,
Under her clothes, about the breasts, under the arms; the
   corners of the cardboard boxes
Cut into the soft flesh; but with a piece of rope for a girdle
   and wound about the shoulders
All was made fast. The mare stood still as if asleep in the
   midst of the water. Then California
Reached out a hand over the stream and fingered her rump;
   the solid wet convexity of it
Shook like the beat of a great heart. "What are you wait-
   ing for?" But the feel of the animal surface
Had wakened a dream, obscured real danger with a dream
   of danger. "What for? For the water-stallion
To break out of the stream, that is what the rump strains for,
   him to come up flinging foam sidewise,
Fore-hooves in air, crush me and the rig and curl over his
   woman." She flung out with the whip then;
The mare plunged forward. The buggy drifted sidelong:
   was she off ground? Swimming? No: by the splashes.
The driver, a mere prehensile instinct, clung to the side-
   irons of the seat and felt the force
But not the coldness of the water, curling over her knees,
   breaking up to the waist
Over her body. They'd turned. The mare had turned up
   stream and was wallowing back into shoal water.
Then California dropped her forehead to her knees, having
   seen nothing, feeling a danger,
And felt the brute weight of a branch of alder, the pendulous
   light leaves brush her bent neck
Like a child's fingers. The mare burst out of water and
   stopped on the slope to the ford. The woman climbed
   down

[15]

Between the wheels and went to her head. "Poor Dora,"
  she called her by her name, "there, Dora. Quietly,"
And led her around, there was room to turn on the margin,
  the head to the gentle thunder of the water.
She crawled on hands and knees, felt for the ruts, and
  shifted the wheels into them. "You can see, Dora.
I can't. But this time you'll go through it." She climbed
  into the seat and shouted angrily. The mare
Stopped, her two forefeet in the water. She touched with
  the whip. The mare plodded ahead and halted.
Then California thought of prayer: "Dear little Jesus,
Dear baby Jesus born to-night, your head was shining
Like silver candles. I've got a baby too, only a girl. You
  had light wherever you walked.
Dear baby Jesus give me light." Light streamed: rose, gold,
  rich purple, hiding the ford like a curtain.
The gentle thunder of water was a noise of wing-feathers,
  the fans of paradise lifting softly.
The child afloat on radiance had a baby face, but the angels
  had birds' heads, hawks' heads,
Bending over the baby, weaving a web of wings about him.
  He held in the small fat hand
A little snake with golden eyes, and California could see
  clearly on the under radiance
The mare's pricked ears, a sharp black fork against the
  shining light-fall. But it dropped; the light of heaven
Frightened poor Dora. She backed; swung up the water,
And nearly oversetting the buggy turned and scrambled back-
  ward; the iron wheel-tires rang on bowlders.

Then California weeping climbed between the wheels. Her
  wet clothes and the toys packed under
Dragged her down with their weight; she stripped off cloak
  and dress and laid the baby's things in the buggy;
Brought Johnny's whisky out from under the seat; wrapped
  all in the dress, bottles and toys, and tied them

[16]

Into a bundle that would sling over her back. She un-
  harnessed the mare, hurting her fingers
Against the swollen straps and the wet buckles. She tied
  the pack over her shoulders, the cords
Crossing her breasts, and mounted. She drew up her shift
  about her waist and knotted it, naked thighs
Clutching the sides of the mare, bare flesh to the wet withers,
  and caught the mane with her right hand,
The looped-up bridle-reins in the other. "Dora, the baby
  gives you light." The blinding radiance
Hovered the ford. "Sweet baby Jesus give us light." Cat-
  aracts of light and Latin singing
Fell through the willows; the mare snorted and reared: the
  roar and thunder of the invisible water;
The night shaking open like a flag, shot with the flashes;
  the baby face hovering; the water
Beating over her shoes and stockings up to the bare thighs;
  and over them, like a beast
Lapping her belly; the wriggle and pitch of the mare swim-
  ming; the drift, the sucking water; the blinding
Light above and behind with not a gleam before, in the
  throat of darkness; the shock of the fore-hooves
Striking bottom, the struggle and surging lift of the haunches.
  She felt the water streaming off her
From the shoulders down; heard the great strain and sob of
  the mare's breathing, heard the horseshoes grind on gravel.
When California came home the dog at the door snuffed
  at her without barking; Christine and Johnny
Both were asleep; she did not sleep for hours, but kindled
  fire and knelt patiently over it,
Shaping and drying the dear-bought gifts for Christmas
  morning.

She hated (she thought) the proud-necked stallion.
He'd lean the big twin masses of his breast on the rail, his
  red-brown eyes flash the white crescents,

She admired him then, she hated him for his uselessness,
    serving nothing
But Johnny's vanity. Horses were too cheap to breed. She
    thought, if he could range in freedom,
Shaking the red-roan mane for a flag on the bare hills.

                                        A man
    brought up a mare in April;
Then California, though she wanted to watch, stayed with
    Christine indoors. When the child fretted
The mother told her once more about the miracle of the
    ford; her prayer to the little Jesus
The Christmas Eve when she was bringing the gifts home;
    the appearance, the lights, the Latin singing,
The thunder of wing-feathers and water, the shining child,
    the cataracts of splendor down the darkness.
"A little baby," Christine asked, "the God is a baby?" "The
    child of God. That was his birthday.
His mother was named Mary: we pray to her too: God came
    to her. He was not the child of a man
Like you or me. God was his father: she was the stallion's
    wife—what did I say—God's wife,"
She said with a cry, lifting Christine aside, pacing the planks
    of the floor. "She is called more blessed
Than any woman. She was so good, she was more loved."
    "Did God live near her house?" "He lives
Up high, over the stars; he ranges on the bare blue hill of
    the sky." In her mind a picture
Flashed, of the red-roan mane shaken out for a flag on the
    bare hills, and she said quickly, "He's more
Like a great man holding the sun in his hand." Her mind
    giving her words the lie, "But no one
Knows, only the shining and the power. The power, the
    terror, the burning fire covered her over . . ."
"Was she burnt up, mother?" "She was so good and lovely,
    she was the mother of the little Jesus.
If you are good nothing will hurt you." "What did she
    think?" "She loved, she was not afraid of the hooves—

Hands that had made the hills and sun and moon, and the
  sea and the great redwoods, the terrible strength,
She gave herself without thinking." "You only saw the
  baby, mother?" "Yes, and the angels about him,
The great wild shining over the black river." Three times
  she had walked to the door, three times returned,
And now the hand that had thrice hung on the knob, full of
  prevented action, twisted the cloth
Of the child's dress that she had been mending. "Oh, Oh,
  I've torn it." She struck at the child and then embraced
  her
Fiercely, the small blond sickly body.
                                       Johnny came in, his face
  reddened as if he had stood
Near fire, his eyes triumphing. "Finished," he said, and
  looked with malice at Christine. "I go
Down valley with Jim Carrier; owes me five dollar, fifteen
  I charge him, he brought ten in his pocket.
Has grapes on the ranch, maybe I take a barrel red wine
  instead of money. Be back to-morrow.
To-morrow night I tell you— Eh, Jim," he laughed over his
  shoulder, "I say to-morrow evening
I show her how the red fellow act, the big fellow. When I
  come home." She answered nothing, but stood
In front of the door, holding the little hand of her daughter,
  in the path of sun between the redwoods,
While Johnny tied the buckskin mare behind Carrier's buggy,
  and bringing saddle and bridle tossed them
Under the seat. Jim Carrier's mare, the bay, stood with
  drooped head and started slowly, the men
Laughing and shouting at her; their voices could be heard
  down the steep road, after the noise
Of the iron-hooped wheels died from the stone. Then one
  might hear the hush of the wind in the tall redwoods,
The tinkle of the April brook, deep in its hollow.
                                       Humanity is the
  start of the race; I say

Humanity is the mold to break away from, the crust to break
    through, the coal to break into fire,
The atom to be split.
                    Tragedy that breaks man's face and a white
    fire flies out of it; vision that fools him
Out of his limits, desire that fools him out of his limits,
    unnatural crime, inhuman science,
Slit eyes in the mask; wild loves that leap over the walls of
    nature, the wild fence-vaulter science,
Useless intelligence of far stars, dim knowledge of the spin-
    ning demons that make an atom,
These break, these pierce, these deify, praising their God
    shrilly with fierce voices: not in a man's shape
He approves the praise, he that walks lightning-naked on the
    Pacific, that laces the suns with planets,
The heart of the atom with electrons: what is humanity in this
    cosmos? For him, the last
Least taint of a trace in the dregs of the solution; for itself,
    the mold to break away from, the coal
To break into fire, the atom to be split.

                    After the child slept, after
    the leopard-footed evening
Had glided oceanward, California turned the lamp to its least
    flame and glided from the house.
She moved sighing, like a loose fire, backward and forward
    on the smooth ground by the door.
She heard the night-wind that draws down the valley like the
    draught in a flue under clear weather
Whisper and toss in the tall redwoods; she heard the tinkle
    of the April brook deep in its hollow.
Cooled by the night the odors that the horses had left behind
    were in her nostrils; the night
Whitened up the bare hill; a drift of coyotes by the river
    cried bitterly against moonrise;
Then California ran to the old corral, the empty one where
    they kept the buckskin mare,

And leaned, and bruised her breasts on the rail, feeling the
   sky whiten.   When the moon stood over the hill
She stole to the house.   The child breathed quietly.   Herself:
   to sleep?   She had seen Christ in the night at Christmas.
The hills were shining open to the enormous night of the
   April moon: empty and empty,
The vast round backs of the bare hills?   If one should ride
   up high might not the Father himself
Be seen brooding His night, cross-legged, chin in hand, squat-
   ting on the last dome?   More likely
Leaping the hills, shaking the red-roan mane for a flag on the
   bare hills.   She blew out the lamp.
Every fiber of flesh trembled with faintness when she came
   to the door; strength lacked, to wander
Afoot into the shining of the hill, high enough, high enough
   . . . the hateful face of a man had taken
The strength that might have served her, the corral was
   empty.   The dog followed her, she caught him by the
   collar,
Dragged him in fierce silence back to the door of the house,
   latched him inside.
                    It was like daylight
Out-doors and she hastened without faltering down the foot-
   path, through the dark fringe of twisted oak-brush,
To the open place in a bay of the hill.   The dark strength of
   the stallion had heard her coming; she heard him
Blow the shining air out of his nostrils, she saw him in the
   white lake of moonlight
Move like a lion along the timbers of the fence, shaking the
   nightfall
Of the great mane; his fragrance came to her; she leaned on
   the fence;
He drew away from it, the hooves making soft thunder in the
   trodden soil.
Wild love had trodden it, his wrestling with the stranger, the
   shame of the day
Had stamped it into mire and powder when the heavy fetlocks

Strained the soft flanks. "Oh, if I could bear you!
If I had the strength. O great God that came down to
   Mary, gently you came. But I will ride him
Up into the hill, if he throws me, if he tramples me, is it not
   my desire
To endure death?" She climbed the fence, pressing her body
   against the rail, shaking like fever,
And dropped inside to the soft ground. He neither threat-
   ened her with his teeth nor fled from her coming,
And lifting her hand gently to the upflung head she caught
   the strap of the headstall,
That hung under the quivering chin. She unlooped the halter
   from the high strength of the neck
And the arch the storm-cloud mane hung with live darkness.
   He stood; she crushed her breasts
On the hard shoulder, an arm over the withers, the other
   under the mass of his throat, and murmuring
Like a mountain dove, "If I could bear you." No way, no
   help, a gulf in nature. She murmured, "Come,
We will run on the hill. O beautiful, O beautiful," and led
   him
To the gate and flung the bars on the ground. He threw
   his head downward
To snuff at the bars; and while he stood, she catching mane
   and withers with all sudden contracture
And strength of her lithe body, leaped, clung hard, and was
   mounted. He had been ridden before; he did not
Fight the weight but ran like a stone falling;
Broke down the slope into the moon-glass of the stream, and
   flattened to his neck
She felt the branches of a buck-eye tree fly over her, saw
   the wall of the oak-scrub
End her world: but he turned there, the matted branches
Scraped her right knee, the great slant shoulders
Laboring the hill-slope, up, up, the clear hill. Desire had
   died in her
At the first rush, the falling like death, but now it revived,

[22]

She feeling between her thighs the labor of the great engine,
the running muscles, the hard swiftness,
She riding the savage and exultant strength of the world.
Having topped the thicket he turned eastward,
Running less wildly; and now at length he felt the halter
when she drew on it; she guided him upward;
He stopped and grazed on the great arch and pride of the
hill, the silent calvary. A dwarfish oakwood
Climbed the other slope out of the dark of the unknown
canyon beyond; the last wind-beaten bush of it
Crawled up to the height, and California slipping from her
mount tethered him to it. She stood then,
Shaking. Enormous films of moonlight
Trailed down from the height. Space, anxious whiteness,
vastness. Distant beyond conception the shining ocean
Lay light like a haze along the ledge and doubtful world's
end. Little vapors gleaming, and little
Darknesses on the far chart underfoot symbolized wood and
valley; but the air was the element, the moon-
Saturate arcs and spires of the air.
                              Here is solitude, here on the
calvary, nothing conscious
But the possible God and the cropped grass, no witness, no
eye but that misformed one, the moon's past fullness.
Two figures on the shining hill, woman and stallion, she
kneeling to him, brokenly adoring.
He cropping the grass, shifting his hooves, or lifting the long
head to gaze over the world,
Tranquil and powerful. She prayed aloud, "O God I am
not good enough, O fear, O strength, I am draggled.
Johnny and other men have had me, and O clean power!
Here am I," she said, falling before him,
And crawled to his hooves. She lay a long while, as if
asleep, in reach of the fore-hooves, weeping. He avoided
Her head and the prone body. He backed at first; but later
plucked the grass that grew by her shoulder.

[28]

The small dark head under his nostrils: a small round stone,
   that smelt human, black hair growing from it:
The skull shut the light in: it was not possible for any eyes
To know what throbbed and shone under the sutures of the
   skull, or a shell full of lightning
Had scared the roan strength, and he'd have broken tether,
   screaming, and run for the valley.
                           The atom bounds-breaking,
Nucleus to sun, electrons to planets, with recognition
Not praying, self-equaling, the whole to the whole, the
   microcosm
Not entering nor accepting entrance, more equally, more ut-
   terly, more incredibly conjugate
With the other extreme and greatness; passionately percep-
   tive of identity. . . .
                     The fire threw up figures
And symbols meanwhile, racial myths formed and dissolved
   in it, the phantom rulers of humanity
That without being are yet more real than what they are
   born of, and without shape, shape that which makes them:
The nerves and the flesh go by shadowlike, the limbs and the
   lives shadowlike, these shadows remain, these shadows
To whom temples, to whom churches, to whom labors and
   wars, visions and dreams are dedicate:
Out of the fire in the small round stone that black moss cov-
   ered, a crucified man writhed up in anguish;
A woman covered by a huge beast in whose mane the stars
   were netted, sun and moon were his eyeballs,
Smiled under the unendurable violation, her throat swollen
   with the storm and blood-flecks gleaming
On the stretched lips; a woman—no, a dark water, split by
   jets of lightning, and after a season
What floated up out of the furrowed water, a boat, a fish, a
   fire-globe?
                  It had wings, the creature,
And flew against the fountain of lightning, fell burnt out of
   the cloud back to the bottomless water . . .

Figures and symbols, castlings of the fire, played in her
brain; but the white fire was the essence,
The burning in the small round shell of bone that black hair
covered, that lay by the hooves on the hilltop.

She rose at length, she unknotted the halter; she walked and
led the stallion; two figures, woman and stallion,
Came down the silent emptiness of the dome of the hill, under
the cataract of the moonlight.

The next night there was moon through cloud. Johnny had
returned half drunk toward evening, and California
Who had known him for years with neither love nor loathing
to-night hating him had let the child Christine
Play in the light of the lamp for hours after her bedtime;
who fell asleep at length on the floor
Beside the dog; then Johnny: "Put her to bed." She gath-
ered the child against her breasts, she laid her
In the next room, and covered her with a blanket. The
window was white, the moon had risen. The mother
Lay down by the child, but after a moment Johnny stood in
the doorway. "Come drink." He had brought home
Two jugs of wine slung from the saddle, part payment for
the stallion's service; a pitcher of it
Was on the table, and California sadly came and emptied her
glass. Whisky, she thought,
Would have erased him till to-morrow; the thin red wine. . . .
"We have a good evening," he laughed, pouring it.
"One glass yet then I show you what the red fellow did."
She moving toward the house-door his eyes
Followed her, the glass filled and the red juice ran over the
table. When it struck the floor-planks
He heard and looked. "Who stuck the pig?" he muttered
stupidly, "here's blood, here's blood," and trailed his
fingers
In the red lake under the lamplight. While he was looking
down the door creaked, she had slipped out-doors,

And he, his mouth curving like a faun's, imagined the chase
   under the solemn redwoods, the panting
And unresistant victim caught in a dark corner. He emptied
   the glass and went out-doors
Into the dappled lanes of moonlight. No sound but the
   April brook's. "Hey Bruno," he called, "find her.
Bruno, go find her." The dog after a little understood and
   quested, the man following.
When California crouching by an oak-bush above the house
   heard them come near she darted
To the open slope and ran down hill. The dog barked at her
   heels, pleased with the game, and Johnny
Followed in silence. She ran down to the new corral, she
   saw the stallion
Move like a lion along the timbers of the fence, the dark
   arched neck shaking the nightfall
Of the great mane; she threw herself prone and writhed
   under the bars, his hooves backing away from her
Made muffled thunder in the soft soil. She stood in the
   midst of the corral, panting, but Johnny
Paused at the fence. The dog ran under it, and seeing the
   stallion move, the woman standing quiet,
Danced after the beast, with white-tooth feints and dashes.
   When Johnny saw the formidable dark strength
Recoil from the dog, he climbed up over the fence.

The child Christine waked when her mother left her
And lay half dreaming, in the half-waking dream she saw
   the ocean come up out of the west
And cover the world, she looked up through clear water at
   the tops of the redwoods. She heard the door creak
And the house empty; her heart shook her body, sitting up on
   the bed, and she heard the dog
And crept toward light, where it gleamed under the crack of
   the door. She opened the door, the room was empty,
The table-top was a red lake under the lamplight. The color
   of it was terrible to her;

She had seen the red juice drip from a coyote's muzzle, her
   father had shot one day in the hills
And carried him home over the saddle: she looked at the rifle
   on the wall-rack: it was not moved:
She ran to the door, the dog was barking and the moon was
   shining: she knew wine by the odor
But the color frightened her, the empty house frightened her,
   she followed down hill in the white lane of moonlight
The friendly noise of the dog. She saw in the big horse's
   corral, on the level shoulder of the hill,
Black on white, the dark strength of the beast, the dancing
   fury of the dog, and the two others.
One fled, one followed; the big one charged, rearing; one fell
   under his fore-hooves. She heard her mother
Scream: without thought she ran to the house, she dragged
   a chair past the red pool and climbed to the rifle,
Got it down from the wall and lugged it somehow through the
   door and down the hillside, under the hard weight
Sobbing. Her mother stood by the rails of the corral, she
   gave it to her. On the far side
The dog flashed at the plunging stallion; in the midst of the
   space the man, slow-moving, like a hurt worm
Crawling, dragged his body by inches toward the fence-line.
   Then California, resting the rifle
On the top rail, without doubting, without hesitance,
Aimed for the leaping body of the dog, and when it stood,
   fired. It snapped, rolled over, lay quiet.
"O mother you've hit Bruno!" "I couldn't see the sights
   in the moonlight," she answered quietly. She stood
And watched, resting the rifle-butt on the ground. The stal-
   lion wheeled, freed from his torment, the man
Lurched up to his knees, wailing a thin and bitter bird's cry,
   and the roan thunder
Struck; hooves left nothing alive but teeth tore up the rem-
   nant. "O mother, shoot, shoot!" Yet California
Stood carefully watching, till the beast having fed all his
   fury stretched neck to utmost, head high,

And wrinkled back the upper lip from the teeth, yawning
  obscene disgust over—not a man—
A smear on the moon-lake earth: then California moved by
  some obscure human fidelity
Lifted the rifle. Each separate nerve-cell of her brain flam-
  ing the stars fell from their places
Crying in her mind: she fired three times before the haunches
  crumpled sidewise, the forelegs stiffening,
And the beautiful strength settled to earth: she turned then
  on her little daughter the mask of a woman
Who has killed God. The night-wind veering, the smell of
  the spilt wine drifted down hill from the house.

THE TOWER BEYOND TRAGEDY

I

You'd never have thought the Queen was Helen's sister—
    Troy's burning-flower from Sparta, the beautiful sea-
    flower
Cut in clear stone, crowned with the fragrant golden mane,
    she the ageless, the uncontaminable—
This Clytemnestra was her sister, low-statured, fierce-lipped,
    not dark nor blond, greenish-gray-eyed,
Sinewed with strength, you saw, under the purple folds of
    the queen-cloak, but craftier than queenly,
Standing between the gilded wooden porch-pillars, great steps
    of stone above the steep street,
Awaiting the King.
                    Most of his men were quartered on the
    town; he, clanking bronze, with fifty
And certain captives, came to the stair. The Queen's men
    were a hundred in the street and a hundred
Lining the ramp, eighty on the great flags of the porch; she
    raising her white arms the spear-butts
Thundered on the stone, and the shields clashed; eight shin-
    ing clarions
Let fly from the wide window over the entrance the wild-
    birds of their metal throats, air-cleaving
Over the King come home. He raised his thick burnt-colored
    beard and smiled; then Clytemnestra,
Gathering the robe, setting the golden-sandaled feet care-
    fully, stone by stone, descended
One half the stair. But one of the captives marred the come-
    liness of that embrace with a cry

[29]

Gull-shrill, blade-sharp, cutting between the purple cloak and
    the bronze plates, then Clytemnestra:
Who was it?   The King answered: A piece of our goods out
    of the snatch of Asia, a daughter of the king,
So treat her kindly and she may come into her wits again.
    Eh, you keep state here my queen.
You've not been the poorer for me.—In heart, in the widowed
    chamber, dear, she pale replied, though the slaves
Toiled, the spearmen were faithful.   What's her name, the
    slave-girl's?
AGAMEMNON   Come up the stair.   They tell me my kinsman's
Lodged himself on you.
CLYTEMNESTRA   Your cousin Ægisthus?   He was out of
    refuge, flits between here and Tiryns.
Dear: the girl's name?
AGAMEMNON   Cassandra.   We've a hundred or so
    other captives; besides two hundred
Rotted in the hulls,—they tell odd stories about you and
    your guest: eh? no matter:—the ships
Ooze pitch and the August road smokes dirt, I smell like an
    old shepherd's goatskin, you'll have bath-water?
CLYTEMNESTRA
They're making it hot.   Come, my lord.   My hands will
    pour it.   (*They enter the palace.*)
CASSANDRA
In the holy city,
In Troy, when the stone was standing walls and the ash
Was painted and carved wood and pictured curtains,
And those lived that are dead, they had caged a den
Of wolves out of the mountain, and I a maiden
Was led to see them: it stank and snarled,
The smell was the smell here, the eyes were the eyes
Of steep Mycenæ: O God guardian of wanderers
Let me die easily.
So cried Cassandra the daughter of King Priam, treading the
    steps of the palace at Mycenæ,

Swaying like a drunken woman, drunk with the rolling of the
ship, and with tears, and with prophecy.
The stair may yet be seen, among the old stones that are
Mycenæ; tall dark Cassandra, the prophetess,
The beautiful girl with whom a God bargained for love, high-
nurtured, captive, shamefully stained
With the ship's filth and the sea's, rolled her dark head upon
her shoulders like a drunken woman
And trod the great stones of the stair. The captives, she
among them, were ranked into a file
On the flagged porch, between the parapet and the spear-
men. The people below shouted for the King,
King Agamemnon, returned conqueror, after the ten years of
battle and death in Asia.
Then cried Cassandra:
Good spearmen you did not kill my father, not you
Violated my mother with the piercing
That makes no life in the womb, not you defiled
My tall blond brothers with the masculine lust
That strikes its loved one standing,
And leaves him what no man again nor a girl
Ever will gaze upon with the eyes of desire:
Therefore you'll tell me
Whether it's an old custom in the Greek country
The cow goring the bull, break the inner door back
And see in what red water how cloaked your King
Bathes, and my brothers are avenged a little.
One said: Captive be quiet. And she: What have I to be
quiet for, you will not believe me.
Such wings my heart spreads when the red runs out of any
Greek, I must let the bird fly. O soldiers
He that mishandled me dies! The first, one of your two
brute Ajaxes, that threw me backward
On the temple flagstones, a hard bride-bed, I enduring him
heard the roofs of my city breaking,
The roar of flames and spearmen: what came to Ajax? Out
of a cloud the loud-winged falcon lightning

Came on him shipwrecked, clapped its wings about him, clung
    to him, the violent flesh burned and the bones
Broke from each other in that passion; and now this one,
    returned safe, the Queen is his lightning.
While she yet spoke a slave with haggard eyes darted from
    the door; there were hushed cries and motions
In the inner dark of the great hall. Then the Queen Clytem-
    nestra issued, smiling. She drew
Her cloak up, for the brooch on the left shoulder was broken;
    the fillet of her hair had come unbound;
Yet now she was queenly at length; and standing at the stair-
    head spoke: Men of Mycenæ, I have made
Sacrifice for the joy this day has brought to us, the King
    come home, the enemy fallen, fallen,
In the ashes of Asia. I have made sacrifice. I made the
    prayer with my own lips, and struck the bullock
With my own hand. The people murmured together, She's
    not a priestess, the Queen is not a priestess,
What has she done there, what wild sayings
Make wing in the Queen's throat?
CLYTEMNESTRA   I have something to tell you.
    Too much joy is a message-bearer of misery.
A little is good; but come too much and it devours us. There-
    fore we give of a great harvest
Sheaves to the smiling Gods; and therefore out of a full cup
    we pour the quarter. No man
Dare take all that God sends him, whom God favors, or de-
    struction
Rides into the house in the last basket. I have been twelve
    years your shepherdess, I the Queen have ruled you
And I am accountable for you.
CASSANDRA
Why should a man kill his own mother?
The cub of the lion being grown
Will fight with the lion, but neither lion nor wolf
Nor the unclean jackal
Bares tooth against the womb that he dropped out of:

Yet I have seen—

CLYTEMNESTRA

Strike that captive woman with your hand, spearman; and
    then if the spirit

Of the she-wolf in her will not quiet, with the butt of the
    spear.

CASSANDRA   —the blade in the child's hand

Enter the breast that the child sucked—that woman's—

The left breast that the robe has dropped from, for the brooch
    is broken,

That very hillock of whiteness, and she crying, she kneel-
    ing—

> (*The spearman who is nearest* CASSANDRA *covers her
> mouth with his hand.*)

CLYTEMNESTRA

My sister's beauty entered Troy with too much gladness.
    They forgot to make sacrifice.

Therefore destruction entered; therefore the daughters of
    Troy cry out in strange dispersals, and this one

Grief has turned mad. I will not have that horror march
    under the lion-gate of Mycenæ

That split the citadel of Priam. Therefore I say I have made
    sacrifice; I have subtracted

A fraction from immoderate joy. For consider, my people,

How unaccountably God has favored the city and brought
    home the army. King Agamemnon,

My dear, my husband, my lord and yours,

Is yet not such a man as the Gods love; but insolent, fierce,
    overbearing, whose folly

Brought many times many great evils

On all the heads and fighting hopes of the Greek force. Why,
    even before the fleet made sail,

While yet it gathered on Bœotian Aulis, this man offended.
    He slew one of the deer

Of the sacred herd of Artemis, out of pure impudence, hunt-
    er's pride that froths in a young boy

Laying nock to string of his first bow: this man, grown, a
   grave king, leader of the Greeks.
The angry Goddess
Blew therefore from the horn of the Trojan shore storm with-
   out end, no slackening, no turn, no slumber
Of the eagle bound to break the oars of the fleet and split the
   hulls venturing: you know what answer
Calchas the priest gave: his flesh must pay whose hand did
   the evil—his flesh! mine also. His? My daughter.
They knew that of my three there was one that I loved.
Blameless white maid, my Iphigenia, whose throat the knife,
Whose delicate soft throat the thing that cuts sheep open was
   drawn across by a priest's hand
And the soft-colored lips drained bloodless
That had clung here—here—Oh!

                    (*Drawing the robe from her breasts.*)
These feel soft, townsmen; these are red at the tips, they
   have neither blackened nor turned marble.
King Agamemnon hoped to pillow his black-haired breast upon
   them, my husband, that mighty conqueror,
Come home with glory. He thought they were still a
   woman's, they appear a woman's. I'll tell you something.
Since fawn slaughtered for slaughtered fawn evened the debt
   these that feel soft and warm are wounding ice,
They ache with their hardness . . .
Shall I go on and count the other follies of the King? The
   insolences to God and man
That brought down plague, and brought Achilles' anger
   against the army? Yet God brought home a remnant
Against all hope: therefore rejoice.
But lest too much rejoicing slay us I have made sacrifice. A
   little girl's brought you over the sea.
What could be great enough for safe return? A sheep's
   death? A bull's? What thank-offering?
All these captives, battered from the ships, bruised with cap-
   tivity, damaged flesh and forlorn minds?

God requires wholeness in the victim. You dare not think
what he demands. I dared. I, I,
Dared.
Men of the Argolis, you that went over the sea and you that
guarded the home coasts
And high stone war-belts of the cities: remember how many
spearmen these twelve years have called me
Queen, and have loved me, and been faithful, and *remain*
faithful. What I bring you is accomplished.

VOICES
King Agamemnon. The King. We will hear the King.

CLYTEMNESTRA   What I bring you is accomplished.
Accept it, the cities are at peace, the ways are safe between
them, the Gods favor us. Refuse it . . .
You will not refuse it . . .

VOICES   The King. We will hear the King. Let us
see the King.

CLYTEMNESTRA
You will not refuse it; I have my faithful. They would run,
the red rivers,
From the gate and by the graves through every crooked street
of the great city, they would run in the pasture
Outside the walls: and on this stair: stemmed at this en-
trance—

CASSANDRA
Ah, sister, do you also behold visions? I was watching red
water—

CLYTEMNESTRA
Be wise, townsmen. As for the King: slaves will bring him
to you when he has bathed; you will see him.
The slaves will carry him on a litter, he has learned Asian
ways in Asia, too great a ruler
To walk, like common spearmen.

CASSANDRA   Who is that, standing behind
you, Clytemnestra? What God
Dark in the doorway?

[85]

CLYTEMNESTRA   Deal *you* with your own demons. You
know what I have done, captive. You know
I am holding lions with my two eyes: if I turn and loose
them . . .

CASSANDRA It is . . . the King. There! There! Ah!

CLYTEMNESTRA
Or if I should make any move to increase confusion. If I
should say for example, Spearman
Kill that woman. I cannot say it this moment; so little as
from one spear wound in your body
A trickle would loose them on us.

CASSANDRA   Yet he stands behind you.
A-ah! I can bear it. I have seen much lately
Worse.

A CAPTAIN (*down the stair; standing forward from his men*)
O Queen, there is no man in the world, but one (if that
one lives), may ask you to speak
Otherwise than you will. You have spoken in riddles to the
people . . .

CASSANDRA   Not me! Why will you choose
Me! I submitted to you living, I was forced, you entered
me . . .

THE CAPTAIN Also there was a slave here,
Whose eyes stood out from his chalk face, came bussing from
the palace postern gate, whimpering
A horrible thing. I killed him. But the men have heard it.

CASSANDRA   You were the king, I was your slave.
Here you see, here, I took the black-haired breast of the bull,
I endured it, I opened my thighs, I suffered
The other thing besides death that you Greeks have to give
us . . .

THE CAPTAIN Though this one raves and you are silent,
O Queen, terrible-eyed . . .

CASSANDRA   That was the slave's part: but this
time . . . dead King . . .
I . . . will . . . not submit. Ah! Ah! No!

If you will steal the body of someone living take your wife's,
   take that soldier's there—

THE CAPTAIN

I pray you Queen command the captive woman be quieted
   in a stone chamber; she increases confusion,
The soldiers cannot know some terrible thing may not have
   happened; your men and the King's grin
Like wolves over the kill, the whole city totters on a sword-
   edge over sudden—

CASSANDRA (*screaming*)

Drive him off me! Pity, pity!
I have no power; I thought when he was dead another man
   would use me, your Greek custom,
Not he, he, newly slain.
He is driving me out, he enters, he possesses, this is my last
   defilement. Ah . . . Greeks . . .
Pity Cassandra!
                    With the voice the spirit seemed to fly out.
   She upflung her shining
Arms with the dreadful and sweet gesture of a woman sur-
   rendering utterly to force and love,
She in the eyes of the people, like a shameless woman, and
   fell writhing, and the dead King's soul
Entered her body. In that respite the Queen:
                                        Captain: and
   you, soldiers, that shift unsoldierly
The weapons that should be upright, at attention, like stiff
   grass-blades: and you, people of Mycenæ:
While this one maddened, and you muttered, echoing together,
   and you, soldier, with anxious questions
Increased confusion: who was it that stood firm, who was it
   that stood silent, who was it that held
With her two eyes the whole city from splitting wide asun-
   der? Your Queen was it? I am your Queen,
And now I will answer what you asked. . . . It is true. . . .
   He has died. . . . I am the Queen.

My little son Orestes will grow up and govern you.

          While she
 spoke the body of Cassandra
Arose among the shaken spears, taller than the spears, and
 stood among the waving spears
Stone-quiet, like a high war-tower in a windy pinewood, but
 deadly to look at, with blind and tyrannous
Eyes; and the Queen: All is accomplished; and if you are
 wise, people of Mycenæ: quietness is wisdom.
No tumult will call home a dead man out of judgment. The
 end is the end. Ah, soldiers! Down spears!
What, now Troy's fallen you think there's not a foreigner in
 the world bronze may quench thirst on? Lion-cubs,
If you will tear each other in the lair happy the wolves,
 happy the hook-nose vultures.
Call the eaters of carrion? I am your queen, I am speaking
 to you, you will hear me out before you whistle
The foul beaks from the mountain nest. I tell you I will
 forget mercy if one man moves now.
I rule you, I.
The Gods have satisfied themselves in this man's death; there
 shall not one drop of the blood of the city
Be shed further. I say the high Gods are content; as for
 the lower,
And the great ghost of the King: my slaves will bring out the
 King's body decently before you
And set it here, in the eyes of the city: spices the ships bring
 from the south will comfort his spirit;
Mycenæ and Tiryns and the shores will mourn him aloud;
 sheep will be slain for him; a hundred beeves
Spill their thick blood into the trenches; captives and slaves
 go down to serve him, yes all these captives
Burn in the ten-day fire with him, unmeasured wine quench
 it, urned in pure gold the gathered ashes
Rest forever in the sacred rock; honored; a conqueror. . . .
 Slaves, bring the King out of the house.

Alas my husband! she cried, clutching the brown strands of
her hair in both her hands, you have left me
A woman among lions! Ah the King's power, ah the King's
victories! Weep for me, Mycenæ!
Widowed of the King!
                        The people stood amazed, like sheep that
    snuff at their dead shepherd, some hunter's
Ill-handled arrow having struck him from the covert, all by
    mischance; he is fallen on the hillside
Between the oak-shadow and the stream; the sun burns his
    dead face, his staff lies by him, his dog
Licks his hand, whining. So, like sheep, the people
Regarded that dead majesty whom the slaves brought out of
    the house on a gold bed, and set it
Between the pillars of the porch. His royal robe covered his
    wounds, there was no stain
Nor discomposure.
                        Then that captain who had spoken before:
    O Queen, before the mourning
The punishment: tell us who has done this. She raised her
    head, and not a woman but a lioness
Blazed at him from her eyes: Dog, she answered, dog of the
    army,
Who said Speak dog, and you dared speak? Justice is mine.
    Then he was silent; but Cassandra's
Body standing tall among the spears, over the parapet, her
    body but not her spirit
Cried with a man's voice: Shall not even the stones of the
    stair, shall not the stones under the columns
Speak, and the towers of the great wall of my city come down
    against the murderess? O Mycenæ
I yearned to night and day under the tents by Troy, O
    Tiryns, O Mycenæ, the door
Of death, and the gate before the door!
CLYTEMNESTRA   That woman lies, or the
    spirit of a lie cries from her. Spearman,
Kill that woman!

But Cassandra's body set its back against the
  parapet, its face
Terribly fronting the raised knife; and called the soldier by
  his name, in the King's voice, saying
Sheathe it; and the knife lowered, and the soldier
Fell on his knees before the King in the woman's body; and
  the body of Cassandra cried from the parapet:
Horrible things, horrible things this house has witnessed: but
  here is the most vile, that hundreds
Of spears are idle while the murderess, Clytemnestra the
  murderess, the snake that came upon me
Naked and bathing, the death that lay with me in bed, the
  death that has borne children to me,
Stands there unslain.

CLYTEMNESTRA   Cowards, if the bawling of that bewildered
  heifer from Troy fields has frightened you
How did you bear the horns of her brothers?   Bring her
  to me.

THE BODY OF CASSANDRA

                              Let no man doubt, men of Mycenæ,
She has yet the knife hid in her clothes, the very blade that
  stabbed her husband and the blood is on it.
Look, she handles it now.   Look, fellows.   The hand under
  the robe.   Slay her not easily, that she-wolf.
Do her no honor with a spear!   Ah!   If I could find the
  word, if I could find it,
The name of her, to say husband-slayer and bed-defiler, bitch
  and wolf-bitch, king's assassin
And beast, beast, beast, all in one breath, in one word: spear-
  men
You would heap your shields over this woman and crush her
  slowly, slowly, while she choked and screamed,
No, you would peel her bare and on the pavement for a bride-
  bed with a spear-butt for husband
Dig the lewd womb until it burst: this for Agamemnon, this
  for Ægisthus—Agh, cowards of the city
Do you stand quiet?

[40]

CLYTEMNESTRA Truly, soldiers,
I think it is he verily. No one could invent the abominable
   voice, the unspeakable gesture,
The actual raging insolence of the tyrant. I am the hand
   ridded the Argolis of him.
I here, I killed him, I, justly.
THE BODY OF CASSANDRA You have heard her, you have
   heard her, she has made confession.
Now if she'll show you the knife too—
CLYTEMNESTRA   Here. I kept it for safety.
And, as that beast said, his blood's yet on it.
Look at it, with so little a key I unlocked the kingdom of de-
   struction. Stand firm, till a God
Lead home this ghost to the dark country
So many Greeks have peopled, through his crimes, his vio-
   lence, his insolence, stand firm till that moment
And through the act of this hand and of this point no man
   shall suffer anything again forever
Of Agamemnon.
THE BODY OF CASSANDRA
              I say if you let this woman live, this crime go
   unpunished, what man among you
Will be safe in his bed? The woman ever envies the man,
   his strength, his freedom, his loves.
Her envy is like a snake beside him, all his life through, her
   envy and hatred: law tames that viper:
Law dies if the Queen die not: the viper is free then,
It will be poison in your meat or a knife to bleed you sleep-
   ing. They fawn and slaver over us
And then we are slain.
CLYTEMNESTRA (to one of the slaves that carried the King's
   body)
              Is my lord Ægisthus
Slain on the way? How long? How long?
                        (To the people) He
   came, fat with his crimes.

Greek valor broke down Troy, your valor, soldiers, and the
  brain of Odysseus, the battle-fury of Achilles,
The stubborn strength of Menelaus, the excellence of you
  all: this dead man here, his pride
Ruined you a hundred times: he helped nowise, he brought
  bitter destruction: but he gathered your glory
For the cloak of his shoulders. I saw him come up the stair,
  I saw my child Iphigenia
Killed for his crime; I saw his harlot, the captive woman
  there, crying out behind him, I saw . . .
I saw . . . I saw . . . how can I speak what crowd of the
  dead faces of the faithful Greeks,
Your brothers, dead of his crimes; those that perished of
  plague and those that died in the lost battles
After he had soured the help of Achilles—for another har-
  lot—those dead faces of your brothers,
Some black with the death-blood, many trampled under the
  hooves of horses, many spotted with pestilence,
Flew all about him, all lamenting, all crying out against him,
  —horrible—horrible—I gave them
Vengeance; and you freedom.
                         (*To the slave*) Go up and look, for
  God's sake, go up to the parapets,
Look toward the mountain. Bring me word quickly, my
  strength breaks,
How can I hold all the Argolis with my eyes forever? I
  alone? Hell cannot hold her dead men,
Keep watch there—send me word by others—go, go!
                         (*To the people*) He
  came triumphing.
Magnificent, abominable, all in bronze.
I brought him to the bath; my hands undid the armor;
My hands poured out the water;
Dead faces like flies buzzed all about us;
He stripped himself before me, loathsome, unclean, with
  laughter;

The labors of the Greeks had made him fat, the deaths of
    the faithful had swelled his belly;
I threw a cloak over him for a net and struck, struck, struck,
Blindly, in the steam of the bath; he bellowed, netted,
And bubbled in the water;
All the stone vault asweat with steam bellowed;
And I undid the net and the beast was dead, and the broad
    vessel
Stank with his blood.

THE BODY OF CASSANDRA
                    The word! the word! O burning mind of God,
If ever I gave you bulls teach me that word, the name for her,
    the name for her!

A SLAVE (*running from the door; to* CLYTEMNESTRA)
My lord Ægisthus has come down the mountain, Queen, he
    approaches the Lion-gate.

CLYTEMNESTRA   It is time.   I am tired now.
Meet him and tell him to come in the postern doorway.

THE CAPTAIN (*on the stair: addressing the soldiers and the
    people below*)
Companions: before God, hating the smell of crimes, crushes
    the city into gray ashes
We must make haste.   Judge now and act.   For the hus-
    band-slayer
I say she must die, let her pay forfeit.   And for the great
    ghost of the King, let all these captives,
But chiefly the woman Cassandra, the crier in a man's voice
    there, be slain upon his pyre to quiet him.
He will go down to his dark place and God will spare the city.
        (*To the soldiers above, on the ramp and the porch*)
                            Comrades: Mycenæ is greater
Than the Queen of Mycenæ.   The King is dead: let the
    Queen die: let the city live.   Comrades,
We suffered something in Asia, on the stranger's coast, labor-
    ing for you.   We dreamed of home there
In the bleak wind and drift of battle; we continued ten years,
    laboring and dying; we accomplished
[43]

The task set us; we gathered what will make all the Greek
    cities glorious, a name forever;
We shared the spoil, taking our share to enrich Mycenæ.
    O but our hearts burned then, O comrades
But our hearts melted when the great oars moved the ships,
    the water carried us, the blue sea-waves
Slid under the black keel; I could not see them, I was blind
    with tears, thinking of Mycenæ.
We have come home.   Behold the dear streets of our longing,
The stones that we desired, the steep ways of the city and
    the sacred doorsteps
Reek and steam with pollution, the accursed vessel
Spills a red flood over the floors.
The fountain of it stands there and calls herself the Queen.
    No queen, no queen, that husband-slayer,
A common murderess.   Comrades join us
We will make clean the city and sweeten it before God.   We
    will mourn together at the King's burying,
And a good year will come, we will rejoice together.
CLYTEMNESTRA   Dog, you dare something.
    Fling no spear, soldiers,
He has a few fools back of him would attempt the stair if
    the dog were slain: I will have no one
Killed out of need.
ONE OF HER MEN ON THE PORCH (*flinging his spear*)
                    Not at him: at you
Murderess!
            But some God, no lover of justice, turned it; the
    great bronze tip grazing her shoulder
Clanged on the stones behind: the gong of a change in the
    dance: now Clytemnestra, none to help her,
One against all, swayed raging by the King's corpse, over
    the golden bed: it is said that a fire
Stood visibly over her head, mixed in the hair, pale flames
    and radiance.
CLYTEMNESTRA   Here am I, thieves, thieves,

Drunkards, here is my breast, a deep white mark for cowards
  to aim at: kings have lain on it.
No spear yet, heroes, heroes?
See, I have no blemish: the arms are white, the breasts are
  deep and white, the whole body is blemishless:
You are tired of your brown wives, draw lots for me, rabble,
  thieves, there is loot here, shake the dice, thieves, a game
  yet!
One of you will take the bronze and one the silver,
One the gold, and one me,
Me Clytemnestra a spoil worth having:
Kings have kissed me, this dead dog was a king, there is an-
  other
King at the gate: thieves, thieves, would not this shining
Breast brighten a sad thief's hut, roll in his bed's filth
Shiningly? You could teach me to draw water at the foun-
  tain,
A dirty child on the other hip: where are the dice? Let me
  throw first, if I throw sixes
I choose my masters: closer you rabble, let me smell you.
Don't fear the knife, it has king's blood on it, I keep it for
  an ornament,
It has shot its sting.
THE BODY OF CASSANDRA. Fools, fools, strike!
Are your hands dead?
CLYTEMNESTRA.   You would see all of me
Before you choose whether to kill or dirtily cherish? If
  what the King's used needs commending
To the eyes of thieves for thieves' use: give me room, give
  me room, fellows, you'll see it is faultless.
The dress . . . there . . .
THE BODY OF CASSANDRA   Fools this wide whore played wife
When she was going about to murder me the King; you, will
  you let her trip you
With the harlot's trick? Strike! Make an end!
CLYTEMNESTRA   I have not my sister's,
  Troy's flame's beauty, but I have something.

[45]

This arm, round, firm, skin without hair, polished like mar-
    ble: the supple-jointed shoulders:
Men have praised the smooth neck, too,
The strong clear throat over the deep wide breasts . . .
THE BODY OF CASSANDRA   She is
    buying an hour: sheep: it may be Ægisthus
Is at the Lion-gate.
CLYTEMNESTRA   If he were here, Ægisthus,
I'd not be the peddler of what trifling charms I have for an
    hour of life yet. You have wolves' eyes:
Yet there is something kindly about the blue ones there—
    yours, young soldier, young soldier. . . . The last,
The under-garment? You won't buy me yet? This dead
    dog,
The King here, never saw me naked: I had the night for
    nurse: turn his head sideways, the eyes
Are only half shut. If I should touch him, and the blood
    came, you'd say I had killed him. Nobody, nobody,
Killed him: his pride burst.
Ah, no one has pity!
I can serve well, I have always envied your women, the pub-
    lic ones.
Who takes me first? Tip that burnt log onto the flagstones,
This will be in a king's bed then. Your eyes are wolves'
    eyes:
So many, so many, so famishing—
I will undo it, handle me not yet, I can undo it . . .
Or I will tear it.
And when it is off me then I will be delivered to you
    beasts . . .
THE BODY OF CASSANDRA
Then strip her and use her to the bones, wear her through,
    kill her with it.
CLYTEMNESTRA
When it is torn
You'll say I am lovely: no one has seen before . . .

It won't tear: I'll slit it with this knife—

(ÆGISTHUS, *with many spearmen, issues from the great
door.* CLYTEMNESTRA *stabs right and left with the
knife; the men are too close to strike her with their
long spears.*)

CLYTEMNESTRA
It's time. Cowards, goats, goats. Here! Ægisthus!

ÆGISTHUS
I am here. What have they done?

CLYTEMNESTRA
Nothing: clear the porch: *I* have done something. Drive
them on the stair!

Three of them I've scarred for life: a rough bridegroom, the
rabble, met a fierce bride.

(*She catches up her robe.*)

I held them with my eyes, hours, hours. I am not tired. . . .
My lord, my lover:

I have killed a twelve-point stag for a present for you: with
my own hands: look, on the golden litter.

You arrive timely.

THE BODY OF CASSANDRA   Tricked, stabbed, shamed, mocked
at, the spoil of a lewd woman, despised

I lie there ready for her back-stairs darling to spit on.
Tricked, stabbed, sunk in the drain

And gutter of time. I that thundered the assault, I that
mustered the Achæans. Cast out of my kingdom,

Cast out of time, out of the light.

CLYTEMNESTRA   One of the captives, dear.
It left its poor wits

Over the sea. If it annoys you I'll quiet it. But post your
sentinels.

All's not safe yet, though I am burning with joy now.

THE BODY OF CASSANDRA   O single-
eyed glare of the sky

Flying southwest to the mountain: sun, through a slave's eyes,

My own broken, I see you this last day; my own darkened,
no dawn forever; the adulterers

Will swim in your warm gold, day after day; the eyes of the
    murderess will possess you;
And I have gone away down: knowing that no God in the
    earth nor sky loves justice; and having tasted
The toad that serves women for heart. From now on may
    all bridegrooms
Marry them with swords. Those that have borne children
Their sons rape them with spears.

CLYTEMNESTRA   More yet, more, more, more,
    while my hand's in? It's not a little
You easily living lords of the sky require of who'd be like
    you, who'd take time in the triumph,
Build joy solid. Do we have to do everything? I have
    killed what I hated:
Kill what I love? The prophetess said it, this dead man
    says it: my little son, the small soft image
That squirmed in my arms be an avenger?—Love, from your
    loins
Seed: I begin new, I will be childless for you. The child
    my son, the child my daughter!
Though I cry I feel nothing.

ÆGISTHUS   O strongest spirit in the world.
    We have dared enough, there is an end to it.
We may pass nature a little, an arrow-flight,
But two shots over the wall you come in a cloud upon the
    feasting Gods, lightning and madness.

CLYTEMNESTRA
Dear: make them safe. They may try to run away, the chil-
    dren. Set spears to watch them: no harm, no harm,
But stab the nurse if they go near a door. Watch them, keep
    the gates, order the sentinels,
While *I* make myself queen over this people again. I can
    do it.

THE BODY OF CASSANDRA   The sun's gone; that glimmer's
The moon of the dead. The dark God calls me. Yes, God,
I'll come in a moment.

CLYTEMNESTRA (*at the head of the great stairs*)

[48]

Soldiers: townsmen: it seems
I am not at the end delivered to you: dogs, for the lion came:
   the poor brown and spotted women
Will have to suffice you. But is it nothing to have come
   within handling distance of the clear heaven
This dead man knew when he was young and God endured
   him? Is it nothing to you?
It is something to me to have felt the fury
And concentration of you: I will not say I am grateful: I
   am not angry: to be desired
Is wine even to a queen. You bathed me in it, from brow
   to foot-sole, I had nearly enough.
But now remember that the dream is over. I am the Queen:
   Mycenæ is my city. If you grin at me
I have spears: also Tiryns and all the country people of the
   Argolis will come against you and swallow you,
Empty out these ways and walls, stock them with better sub-
   jects. A rock nest for new birds here, townsfolk:
You are not essential.
THE BODY OF CASSANDRA. I hear him calling through the she-
   wolf's noise, Agamemnon, Agamemnon,
The dark God calls. Some old king in a fable is it?
CLYTEMNESTRA   So choose.
   What choices? To reënter my service
Unpunished, no thought of things past, free of conditions . . .
Or—dine at this man's table, have new mouths made in you
   to eat bronze with.
THE BODY OF CASSANDRA Who is Agamemnon?
CLYTEMNESTRA
You letting go of the sun: is it dark the land you are run-
   ning away to?
THE BODY OF CASSANDRA It is dark.
CLYTEMNESTRA   Is it sorrowful?
THE BODY OF CASSANDRA
There is nothing but misery.
CLYTEMNESTRA   Has any man ever come back
   thence? Hear *me*, not the dark God.

CLYTEMNESTRA

Go then, go, go down. You will not choose to follow him,
   people of the rock-city? No one
Will choose to follow him. I have killed: it is easy: it may
   be I shall kill nearer than this yet:
But not you, townsfolk, you will give me no cause; I want
   security; I want service, not blood.
I have been desired of the whole city, publicly; I want serv-
   ice, not lust. You will make no sign
Of your submission; you will not give up your weapons;
   neither shall your leaders be slain;
And he that flung the spear, I have forgotten his face.
   ÆGISTHUS (entering)   Dearest,
   they have gone, the nurse and the children,
No one knows where.
   CLYTEMNESTRA   I am taming this people: send men after
   them. If any harm comes to the children
Bring me tokens. I will not be in doubt, I will not have the
   arch fall on us. I dare
What no one dares. I envy a little the dirty mothers of the
   city. O, O!
Nothing in me hurts. I have animal waters in my eyes, but
   the spirit is not wounded. Electra and Orestes
Are not to live when they are caught. Bring me sure tokens.
   CASSANDRA   Who is this woman like a beacon
Lit on the stair, who are these men with dogs' heads?
I have ranged time and seen no sight like this one.
   CLYTEMNESTRA
Have you returned, Cassandra? . . . The dead king has gone
   down to his place, we may bury his leavings.
   CASSANDRA
I have witnessed all the wars to be; I am not sorrowful
For one drop from the pail of desolation
Spilt on my father's city; they were carrying it forward
To water the world under the latter starlight.
   CLYTEMNESTRA (to her slaves)

Take up the poles of the bed; reverently; careful on the stair;
  give him to the people. (*To the people.*) O soldiers
This was your leader; lay him with honor in the burial-
  chapel; guard him with the spears of victory;
Mourn him until to-morrow, when the pyre shall be built.
Ah, King of men, sleep, sleep, sleep!
. . . But when shall I? . . . They are after their corpse, like
  dogs after the butcher's cart. Cleomenes, that captain
With the big voice: Neobulus was the boy who flung the spear
  and missed. *I* shall not miss
When spear-flinging-time comes. . . . Captive woman, you
  have seen the future, tell me my fortune.

              (ÆGISTHUS *comes from the doorway.*)
                                        Ægisthus,
Have your hounds got them?
ÆGISTHUS   I've covered every escape with
  men, they'll not slip through me. But commanded
To bring them here living.
CLYTEMNESTRA   That's hard: tigresses don't do it:
  I have some strength yet: don't speak of it
And I shall do it.
ÆGISTHUS   It is a thing not to be done: we'll guard
  them closely: but mere madness
Lies over the wall of too-much.
CLYTEMNESTRA   King of Mycenæ, new-crowned
  king, who was your mother?
ÆGISTHUS   Pelopia.
What mark do you aim at?
CLYTEMNESTRA   And your father?
ÆGISTHUS   Thyestes.
CLYTEMNESTRA   And her father?
ÆGISTHUS   The
  same man, Thyestes.
CLYTEMNESTRA
See, dearest, dearest? They love what men call crime, they
  have taken her crime to be the king of Mycenæ.

Here is the stone garden of the plants that pass nature: there
  is no too-much here: the monstrous
Old rocks want monstrous roots to serpent among them. I
  will have security. I'd burn the standing world
Up to this hour and begin new. You think I am too much
  used for a new brood? Ah, lover,
I have fountains in me. I had a fondness for the brown
  cheek of that boy, the curl of his lip,
The widening blue of the doomed eyes . . . I will be spared
  nothing. Come in, come in, they'll have news for us.

CASSANDRA

If anywhere in the world
Were a tower with foundations, or a treasure-chamber
With a firm vault, or a walled fortress
That stood on the years, not staggering, not moving
As the mortar were mixed with wine for water
And poppy for lime: they reel, they are all drunkards,
The piled strengths of the world: no pyramid
In bitter Egypt in the desert
But skips at moonrise; no mountain
Over the Black Sea in awful Caucasus
But whirls like a young kid, like a bud of the herd,
Under the hundredth star: I am sick after steadfastness
Watching the world cataractlike
Pour screaming onto steep ruins: for the wings of prophecy
God once my lover give me stone sandals
Planted on stone: he hates me, the God, he will never
Take home the gift of the bridleless horse
The stallion, the unbitted stallion: the bed
Naked to the sky on Mount Ida,
The soft clear grass there,
Be blackened forever, may vipers and Greeks
In that glen breed
Twisting together, where the God
Come golden from the sun
Gave me for a bride-gift prophecy and I took it for a treasure:
I a fool, I a maiden,

[52]

I would not let him touch me though love of him maddened
    me
Till he fed me that poison, till he planted that fire in me,
The girdle flew loose then.

The Queen considered this rock, she gazed on the great stone
    blocks of Mycenæ's acropolis;
Monstrous they seemed to her, solid they appeared to her,
    safe rootage for monstrous deeds: Ah fierce one
Who knows who laid them for a snare? What people in the
    world's dawn breathed on chill air and the vapor
Of their breath seemed stone and has stood and you dream
    it is established? These also are a foam on the stream
Of the falling of the world: there is nothing to lay hold on:
No crime is a crime, the slaying of the King was a meeting
    of two bubbles on the lip of the cataract,
One winked . . . and the killing of your children would be
    nothing: I tell you for a marvel that the earth is a dancer,
The grave dark earth is less quiet than a fool's fingers,
That old one, spinning in the emptiness, blown by no wind
    in vain circles, light-witted and a dancer.
CLYTEMNESTRA (*entering*)
You are prophesying: prophesy to a purpose, captive woman.
    My children, the boy and the girl,
Have wandered astray, no one can find them.
CASSANDRA   Shall I tell the
    lioness
Where meat is, or the she-wolf where the lambs wander
    astray?
CLYTEMNESTRA But look into the darkness
And foam of the world: the boy has great tender blue eyes,
    brown hair, disdainful lips, you'll know him
By the gold stripe bordering his garments; the girl's eyes are
    my color, white her clothing—
CASSANDRA   Millions
Of shining bubbles burst and wander
On the stream of the world falling . . .
            [58]

CLYTEMNESTRA   These are my children!

CASSANDRA   I see
mountains, I see no faces.

CLYTEMNESTRA
Tell me and I make you free; conceal it from me and a sol-
dier's spear finishes the matter.

CASSANDRA
I am the spear's bride, I have been waiting, waiting for that
ecstasy—

CLYTEMNESTRA (*striking her*) Live then.   It will not be un-
painful.   (CLYTEMNESTRA *goes in*.)

CASSANDRA
O fair roads north where the land narrows
Over the mountains between the great gulfs,
O that I too with the King's children
Might wander northward hand in hand.
Mine are worse wanderings:
They will shelter on Mount Parnassus,
For me there is no mountain firm enough,
The storms of light beating on the headlands,
The storms of music undermine the mountains, they stumble
    and fall inward,
Such music the stars
Make in their courses, the vast vibration
Plucks the iron heart of the earth like a harp-string.
Iron and stone core, O stubborn axle of the earth, you also
Dissolving in a little time like salt in water,
What does it matter that I have seen Macedon
Roll all the Greek cities into one billow and strand in Asia
The anthers and bracts of the flower of the world?
That I have seen Egypt and Nineveh
Crumble, and a Latian village
Plant the earth with javelins? It made laws for all men,
    it dissolved like a cloud.
I have also stood watching a storm of wild swans
Rise from one river-mouth . . . O force of the earth rising,
O fallings of the earth: forever no rest, not forever

[54]

From the wave and the trough, from the stream and the slack,
  from growth and decay: O vulture-
Pinioned, my spirit, one flight yet, last, longest, unguided,
Try into the gulf,
Over Greece, over Rome, you have space O my spirit for the
  years

II

Are not few of captivity: how many have I stood here
Among the great stones, while the Queen's people
Go in and out of the gate, wearing light linen
For summer and the wet spoils of wild beasts
In the season of storms: and the stars have changed, I have
  watched
The grievous and unprayed-to constellations
Pile steaming spring and patient autumn
Over the enduring walls: but you over the walls of the
  world,
Over the unquieted centuries, over the darkness-hearted
Millenniums wailing thinly to be born, O vulture-pionioned
Try into the dark,
Watch the north spawn white bodies and red-gold hair,
Race after race of beastlike warriors; and the cities
Burn, and the cities build, and new lands be uncovered
In the way of the sun to his setting . . . go on farther,
  what profit
In the wars and the toils? but I say
Where are prosperous people my enemies are, as you pass
  them O my spirit
Curse Athens for the joy and the marble, curse Corinth
For the wine and the purple, and Syracuse
For the gold and the ships; but Rome, Rome,
With many destructions for the corn and the laws and the
  javelins, the insolence, the threefold
Abominable power: pass the humble
And the lordships of darkness, but far down
Smite Spain for the blood on the sunset gold, curse France

[55]

For the fields abounding and the running rivers, the lights
in the cities, the laughter, curse England
For the meat on the tables and the terrible gray ships, for
old laws, far dominions, there remains
A mightier to be cursed and a higher for malediction
When America has eaten Europe and takes tribute of Asia,
when the ends of the world grow aware of each other
And are dogs in one kennel, they will tear
The master of the hunt with the mouths of the pack: new
fallings, new risings, O winged one
No end of the fallings and risings? An end shall be surely,
Though unnatural things are accomplished, they breathe in
the sea's depth,
They swim in the air, they bridle the cloud-leaper lightning
to carry their messages:
Though the eagles of the east and the west and the falcons
of the north were not quieted, you have seen a white
cloth
Cover the lands from the north and the eyes of the lands
and the claws of the hunters,
The mouths of the hungry with snow
Were filled, and their claws
Took hold upon ice in the pasture, a morsel of ice was their
catch in the rivers,
That pure white quietness
Waits on the heads of the mountains, not sleep but death,
will the fire
Of burnt cities and ships in that year warm you my enemies?
The frost, the old frost,
Like a cat with a broken-winged bird it will play with you,
It will nip and let go; you will say it is gone, but the next
Season it increases: O clean, clean,
White and most clean, colorless quietness,
Without trace, without trail, without stain in the garment,
drawn down
From the poles to the girdle. . . . I have known one Godhead

To my sore hurt: I am growing to come to another: O grave
and kindly
Last of the lords of the earth, I pray you lead my substance
Speedily into another shape, make me grass, Death, make
me stone,
Make me air to wander free between the stars and the
peaks; but cut humanity
Out of my being, that is the wound that festers in me,
Not captivity, not my enemies: you will heal the earth also,
Death, in your time; but speedily Cassandra.
You rock-fleas hopping in the clefts of Mycenæ,
Suckers of blood, you carrying the scepter farther, Persian,
Emathian,
Roman and Mongol and American, and you half-gods
Indian and Syrian and the third, emperors of peace, I have
seen on what stage
You sing the little tragedy; the column of the ice that was
before on one side flanks it,
The column of the ice to come closes it up on the other:
audience nor author
I have never seen yet: I have heard the silence: it is I
Cassandra,
Eight years the bitter watch-dog of these doors,
Have watched a vision
And now approach to my end.   Eight years I have seen
the phantoms
Walk up and down this stair; and the rocks groan in the
night, the great stones move when no man sees them.
And I have forgotten the fine ashlar masonry of the courts
of my father. I am not Cassandra
But a counter of sunrises, permitted to live because I am
crying to die; three thousand,
Pale and red, have flowed over the towers in the wall since
I was here watching; the deep east widens,
The cold wind blows, the deep earth sighs, the dim gray
finger of light crooks at the morning star.

The palace feasted late and sleeps with its locked doors; the
    last drunkard from the alleys of the city
Long has reeled home. Whose foot is this then, what
    phantom
Toils on the stair?
A VOICE BELOW   Is someone watching above? Good sentinel
    I am only a girl beggar.
I would sit on the stair and hold my bowl.
CASSANDRA   I here eight
    years have begged for a thing and not received it.
THE VOICE
You are not a sentinel? You have been asking some great
    boon, out of all reason.
CASSANDRA   No: what the meanest
Beggar disdains to take.
THE GIRL BEGGAR   Beggars disdain nothing: what is it
    that they refuse you?
CASSANDRA   What's given
Even to the sheep and to the bullock.
THE GIRL   Men give them salt,
    grass they find out for themselves.
CASSANDRA   Men give them
The gift that you though a beggar have brought down from
    the north to give my mistress.
THE GIRL   You speak riddles.
I am starving, a crust is my desire.
CASSANDRA   Your voice is young
    though winds have hoarsened it, your body appears
Flexible under the rags: have you some hidden sickness, the
    young men will not give you silver?
THE GIRL
I have a sickness: I will hide it until I am cured. You are
    not a Greek woman?
CASSANDRA   But you
Born in Mycenæ return home. And you bring gifts from
    Phocis: for my once master who's dead

[58]

Vengeance; and for my mistress peace, for my master the
    King peace, and, by-shot of the doom's day,
Peace for me also. But I have prayed for it.

THE GIRL   I know you, I
    knew you before you spoke to me, captive woman,
And I unarmed will kill you with my hands if you babble
    prophecies.
That peace you have prayed for, I will bring it to you
If you utter warnings.

CASSANDRA   To-day I shall have peace, you cannot
    tempt me, daughter of the Queen, Electra.
Eight years ago I watched you and your brother going north
    to Phocis: the Queen saw knowledge of you
Move in my eyes: I would not tell her where you were when
    she commanded me: I will not betray you
To-day either: it is not doleful to me
To see before I die generations of destruction enter the
    doors of Agamemnon.
Where is your brother?

ELECTRA   Prophetess: you see all: I will tell
    you nothing.

CASSANDRA   He has well chosen his ambush,
It is true Ægisthus passes under that house to-day, to hunt
    in the mountain.

ELECTRA   Now I remember
Your name. Cassandra.

CASSANDRA   Hush: the gray has turned yellow,
    the standing beacons
Stream up from the east; they stir there in the palace;
    strange, is it not, the dawn of one's last day's
Like all the others? Your brother would be fortunate if
    to-day were also
The last of his.

ELECTRA   He will endure his destinies; and Cassandra
    hers; and Electra mine.
He has been for years like one tortured with fire: this day
    will quench it.

CASSANDRA They are opening the gates: beg now.
To your trade, beggar-woman.
THE PORTER (*coming out*) Eh, pillar of miseries,
You still on guard there? Like a mare in a tight stall, never
  lying down. What's this then?
A second ragged one? This at least can bend in the middle
  and sit on a stone.
ELECTRA Dear gentleman
I am not used to it, my father is dead and hunger forces
  me to beg, a crust or a penny.
THE PORTER
This tall one's licensed in a manner. I think they'll not let
  two bundles of rag
Camp on the stair: but if you'd come to the back door and
  please me nicely: with a little washing
It'd do for pastime.
ELECTRA I was reared gently: I will sit here, the
  King will see me,
And none mishandle me.
THE PORTER I bear no blame for you.
I have not seen you: you came after the gates were opened.
  (*He goes in.*)
CASSANDRA
O blossom of fire, bitter to men,
Watchdog of the woeful days,
How many sleepers
Bathing in peace, dreaming themselves delight,
All over the city, all over the Argolid plain, all over the
  dark earth,
(Not me, a deeper draught of peace
And darker waters alone may wash me)
Do you, terrible star, star without pity,
Wolf of the east, waken to misery.
To the wants unaccomplished, to the eating desires,
To unanswered love, to hunger, to the hard edges
And mold of reality, to the whips of their masters.
They had flown away home to the happy darkness,

[60]

They were safe until sunrise.

(*King Ægisthus, with his retinue, comes from the great door.*)

ÆGISTHUS

Even here, in the midst of the city, the early day
Has a clear savor. (*To* ELECTRA) What, are you miserable,
   holding the bowl out?
We'll hear the lark to-day in the wide hills and smell the
   mountain. I'd share happiness with you.
What's your best wish, girl beggar?

ELECTRA   It is covered, my lord,
   how should a beggar
Know what to wish for beyond a crust and a dark corner and
   a little kindness?

ÆGISTHUS   Why do you tremble?

ELECTRA

I was reared gently; my father is dead.

ÆGISTHUS   Stand up: will you
   take service here in the house? What country
Bred you gently and proved ungentle to you?

ELECTRA   I have wan-
   dered north from the Eurotas, my lord,
Begging at farmsteads.

ÆGISTHUS   The Queen's countrywoman then,
   she'll use you kindly. She'll be coming
In a moment, then I'll speak for you.—Did you bid them
   yoke the roans into my chariot, Menalcas,
The two from Orchomenus?

ONE OF THE RETINUE   Yesterday evening, my lord,
I sent to the stable.

ÆGISTHUS   They cost a pretty penny, we'll see how
   they carry it.—She's coming: hold up your head, girl.

(CLYTEMNESTRA, *with two serving-women, comes from the door.*)

CLYTEMNESTRA

Good hunt, dearest. Here's a long idle day for me to look
   to. Kill early, come home early.

[61]

ÆGISTHUS

There's a poor creature on the step who's been reared nicely
   and slipped into misery. I said you'd feed her,
And maybe find her a service. Farewell, sweet one.

CLYTEMNESTRA Where did she come from? How long have
   you been here?

ÆGISTHUS She says she has begged her way up from Sparta.
   The horses are stamping on the cobbles, good-by, good-by.
      (*He goes down the stair with his huntsmen.*)

CLYTEMNESTRA Good-by, dearest. Well. Let me see your
   face.

ELECTRA It is filthy to look at. I am ashamed.

CLYTEMNESTRA (*to one of her serving-women*) Leucippe
   do you think this is a gayety of my lord's, he's not used
   to be so kindly to beggars?
—Let me see your face.

LEUCIPPE She is very dirty, my lady. It is possible one
   of the house-boys . . .

CLYTEMNESTRA I say draw that rag back, let me see your
   face. I'd have him whipped then.

ELECTRA It was only in hope that someone would put a
   crust in the bowl, your majesty, for I am starving. I
   didn't think your majesty would see me.

CLYTEMNESTRA Draw back the rag.

ELECTRA I am very faint and starving but I will go down;
   I am ashamed.

CLYTEMNESTRA Stop her, Corinna. Fetch the porter, Leu-
   cippe. You will not go so easily. (ELECTRA *sinks down
   on the steps and lies prone, her head covered.*) I am
   aging out of queenship indeed, when even the beggars
   refuse my bidding. (LEUCIPPE *comes in with the porter.*)
   You have a dirty stair, porter. How long has this been
   here?

THE PORTER O my lady it has crept up since I opened
   the doors, it was not here when I opened the doors.

CLYTEMNESTRA Lift it up and uncover its face. What is
   that cry in the city? Stop: silent: I heard a cry . . .

[62]

Prophetess, your nostrils move like a dog's, what is that
    shouting? . . .
I have grown weak, I am exhausted, things frighten me . . .
Tell her to be gone, Leucippe, I don't wish to see her, I
    don't wish to see her.
    (ELECTRA *rises*.)
ELECTRA Ah, Queen, I will show you my face.
CLYTEMNESTRA No . . . no . . . be gone.
ELECTRA (*uncovering her face*)
Mother: I have come home: I am humbled. This house keeps
    a dark welcome
For those coming home out of far countries.
CLYTEMNESTRA   I won't look: how
    could I know anyone? I am old and shaking.
He said, Over the wall beyond nature
Lightning, and the laughter of the Gods. I did not cross it,
    I will not kill what I gave life to.
Whoever you are, go, go, let me grow downward to the grave
    quietly now.
ELECTRA   I cannot
Go: I have no other refuge. Mother! Will you not kiss me,
    will you not take me into the house,
Your child once, long a wanderer? Electra my name. I
    have begged my way from Phocis, my brother is dead
    there,
Who used to care for me.
CLYTEMNESTRA   Who is dead, who?
ELECTRA   My brother
    Orestes,
Killed in a court quarrel.
CLYTEMNESTRA (*weeping*) Oh, you lie! The widening blue
    blue eyes,
The little voice of the child . . . Liar.
ELECTRA   It is true. I have
    wept long, on every mountain. You, mother,
Have only begun weeping. Far off, in a far country, no fit
    burial . . .

[68]

CLYTEMNESTRA   And do you bringing

Bitterness . . . or lies . . . . look for a welcome?   I have
   only loved two:

The priest killed my daughter for a lamb on a stone and
   now you say the boy too . . . dead, dead?

The world's full of it, a shoreless lake of lies and floating
   rumors . . . pack up your wares, peddler,

Too false for a queen.   Why, no, if I believed you . . .
   Beast, treacherous beast, that shouting comes nearer,

What's in the city?

ELECTRA   I am a stranger, I know nothing of the
   city, I know only

My mother hates me, and Orestes my brother

Died pitifully, far off.

CLYTEMNESTRA   Too many things, too many things call
   me, what shall I do?   Electra,

Electra help me.   This comes of living softly, I had a lion's
   strength

Once.

ELECTRA   Me for help?   I am utterly helpless, I had help
   in my brother and he is dead in Phocis.

Give me refuge: but each of us two must weep for herself,
   one sorrow.   An end of the world were on us

What would it matter to us weeping?   Do you remember
   him,

Mother, mother?

CLYTEMNESTRA   I have dared too much: never dare any-
   thing, Electra, the ache is afterward,

At the hour it hurts nothing.   Prophetess, you lied.

You said he would come with vengeance on me: but now he is
   dead, this girl says: and because he was lovely, blue-
   eyed,

And born in a most unhappy house I will believe it.   But the
   world's fogged with the breath of liars,

And if she has laid a net for me . . .

I'll call up the old lioness lives yet in my body, I have dared,
   I have dared, and tooth and talon

[64]

Carve a way through. Lie to me?

ELECTRA   Have I endured for
   months, with feet bleeding, among the mountains,
Between the great gulfs alone and starving, to bring you a
   lie now? I know the worst of you, I looked for the
   worst,
Mother, mother, and have expected nothing but to die of
   this home-coming: but Orestes
Has entered the cave before; he is gathered up in a lonely
   mountain quietness, he is guarded from angers
In the tough cloud that spears fall back from.

CLYTEMNESTRA   Was he still
   beautiful? The brown mothers down in the city
Keep their brats about them; what it is to live high! Oh!
Tell them down there, tell them in Tiryns,
Tell them in Sparta,
That water drips through the Queen's fingers and trickles
   down her wrists, for the boy, for the boy
Born of her body, whom she, fool, fool, fool,
Drove out of the world. Electra,
Make peace with me.
Oh, Oh, Oh!
I have labored violently all the days of my life for noth-
   ing—nothing—worse than anything—this death
Was a thing I wished. See how they make fools of us.
Amusement for them, to watch us labor after the thing that
   will tear us in pieces. . . . Well, strength's good.
I am the Queen; I will gather up my fragments
And not go mad now.

ELECTRA   Mother, what are the men
With spears gathering at the stair's foot? Not of Mycenæ
   by their armor, have you mercenaries
Wanting pay? Do they serve . . . Ægisthus?

CLYTEMNESTRA   What men? I
   seem not to know . . .
Who has laid a net for me, what fool
For me, me? Porter, by me.

Leucippe, my guards; into the house, rouse them. I am sorry for him,
I am best in storm. You, Electra?
The death you'll die, my daughter. Guards, out! Was it a lie? No matter, no matter, no matter,
Here's peace. Spears, out, out! They bungled the job making me a woman. Here's youth come back to me,
And all the days of gladness.

LEUCIPPE (*running back from the door*) O, Queen, strangers . . .

ORESTES (*a sword in his hand, with spearmen following, comes from the door*) Where is that woman
The Gods utterly hate?

ELECTRA   Brother: let her not speak, kill quickly. Is the other one safe now?

ORESTES   That dog
Fell under his chariot, we made sure of him between the wheels and the hooves, squealing. Now for this one.

CLYTEMNESTRA
Wait. I was weeping, Electra will tell you, my hands are wet still,
For your blue eyes that death had closed she said away up in Phocis. I die now, justly or not
Is out of the story, before I die I'd tell you—wait, child, wait. Did I quiver
Or pale at the blade? I say, caught in a net, netted in by my enemies, my husband murdered,
Myself to die, I am joyful knowing she lied, you live, the only creature
Under all the spread and arch of daylight
That I love, lives.

ELECTRA   The great fangs drawn fear craftiness now, kill quickly.

CLYTEMNESTRA   As for her, the wife of a shepherd
Suckled her, but you
These very breasts nourished: rather one of your northern spearmen do what's needful; not you

[66]

Draw blood where you drew milk. The Gods endure much,
   but beware them.

ORESTES   This, a God in his temple
Openly commanded.

CLYTEMNESTRA   Ah, child, child, who has mistaught you and
   who has betrayed you? What voice had the God?
How was it different from a man's and did you see him?
   Who sent the priest presents? They fool us,
And the Gods let them. No doubt also the envious King
   of Phocis has lent you counsel as he lent you
Men: let one of them do it. Life's not jewel enough
That I should plead for it: this much I pray, for your sake,
   not with your hand, not with your hand, or the memory
Will so mother you, so glue to you, so embracing you,
Not the deep sea's green day, no cleft of a rock in the bed
   of the deep sea, no ocean of darkness
Outside the stars, will hide nor wash you. What is it to me
   that I have rejoiced knowing you alive,
O child, O precious to me, O alone loved, if now dying by
   my manner of death
I make nightmare the heir, nightmare, horror, in all I have
   of you;
And you haunted forever, never to sleep dreamless again,
   never to see blue cloth
But the red runs over it; fugitive of dreams, madman at
   length, the memory of a scream following you houndlike,
Inherit Mycenæ? Child, for this has not been done before,
   there is no old fable, no whisper
Out of the foundation, among the people that were before
   our people, no echo has ever
Moved among these most ancient stones, the monsters here,
   nor stirred under any mountain, nor fluttered
Under any sky, of a man slaying his mother. Sons have
   killed fathers—

ORESTES   And a woman her son's father—

[67]

CLYTEMNESTRA

O many times: and these old stones have seen horrors: a
house of madness and blood
I married into: and worse was done on this rock among the
older people before: but not this,
Not the son his mother; this the silent ones,
The old hard ones, the great bearers of burden have not seen yet,
Nor shall, to-day nor yet to-morrow, nor ever in the world.
Let her do it, it is not unnatural,
The daughter the mother; the little liar there,
Electra do it. Lend her the blade.

ELECTRA   Brother though the great
house is silent hark the city,
That buzzes like the hive one has dipped a wand in. End
this. Then look to our safety.

ORESTES   Dip in my sword
Into my fountain? Did I truly, little and helpless,
Lie in the arms, feed on the breast there?

ELECTRA   Another, a greater,
lay in them, another kissed the breast there,
You forget easily, the breaker of Asia, the over-shadower, the
great memory, under whose greatness
We have hung like hawks under a storm, from the begin-
ning,—and he when this poison destroyed him
Was given no room to plead in.

ORESTES   Dip my wand into my foun-
tain?

CLYTEMNESTRA   Men do not kill the meanest
Without defence heard—

ELECTRA   Him—Agamemnon?

CLYTEMNESTRA   But you, O my
son, my son,
Molded in me, made of me, made of my flesh, built with my
blood, fed with my milk, my child
I here, I and no other, labored to bear, groaning—

ELECTRA   This that
makes beastlike lamentation

Hunted us to slay us, we starving in the thicket above the
    stream three days and nights watched always
Her hunters with spears beating the field: prophetess was
    it for love that she looked after us?

CASSANDRA   That love
The King had tasted; that was her love.

ELECTRA   And mourning for
    our father on the mountain we judged her;
And the God condemned her, what more, what more? Strike.

ORESTES If they'd give me time, the pack there—how can I
    think,
And all the whelps of Mycenæ yelling at the stair-foot?
    Decision: a thing to be decided:
The arm's lame, dip in, dip in? Shut your mouths, rabble.

CLYTEMNESTRA There is one thing no man can do.

ORESTES   What, enter
    his fountain?

ELECTRA
O coward!

ORESTES I will be passive, I'm blunted. She's not this fel-
    low's mother.

ELECTRA   O spearman, spearman, do it!
One stroke: it is just.

THE SPEARMAN   As for me, my lord . . .

CLYTEMNESTRA (*calling loudly*)   Help, help,
    men of Mycenæ, to your Queen. Break them.
Rush the stair, there are only ten hold it. Up, up, kill.

ORESTES I will kill.

CLYTEMNESTRA (*falling on her knees*) Child,
Spare me, let me live! Child! Ai! . . .

ELECTRA   You have done well.

ORESTES I have done . . . I have done . . .
Who ever saw such a flow . . . was I made out of this, I'm
    not red, am I?
See, father?
It was someone else did it but I told him to. Drink, drink,
    dog. Drink dog.

He reaches up a tongue between the stones, lapping it. So
    thirsty old dog, uh?
Rich and sticky.

CLYTEMNESTRA (*raising herself a little*) Sleep . . . for me
    . . . yes.
Not you . . . any more . . . Orestes . . . I shall be there.
    you will beg death . . . vainly as I have begged . . .
    life. Ah . . . beast that I unkennelled! (*She dies.*)

ORESTES (*crouching by her*) Ooh . . . Ooh . . .

ELECTRA
The face is lean and terrible. Orestes!
They are fighting on the stair. Man yourself. Come. Pick
    up the sword.
Let her be, two of ours are down, they yield on the stair.
    Stand up, speak or fight, speak to the people
Or we go where she is.

ORESTES   There's a red and sticky sky that
    you can touch here.
And though it's unpleasant we are at peace.

ELECTRA (*catching up the sword*)   Agamemnon failed
    here. Not in me. Hear, Mycenæans.
I am Agamemnon's daughter, we have avenged him, the
    crime's paid utterly.
You have not forgotten the great King—what, in eight years?
    I am Electra, I am his daughter.
My brother is Orestes. My brother is your king and has
    killed his murderers. The dog Ægisthus is dead,
And the Queen is dead: the city is at peace.

ORESTES (*standing up*)   Must I dip my
    wand into my fountain, give it to me.
The male plaything. (*He catches* ELECTRA'S *arm, snatching
    at the sword.*)

ELECTRA   For what? Be quiet, they have heard me.
ORESTES You said I must do it, I will do it.

ELECTRA   It is done!
Brother, brother? (ORESTES *takes the sword from her by
    force.*) O Mycenæ

With this sword he did justice, he let it fall, he has retaken
it,
He is your King.

ORESTES   Whom must I pierce, the girl that plotted
with me in the mountain? There was someone to kill . . .
Sweet Electra?

ELECTRA   It is done, it is finished!

CASSANDRA   The nearest, the most
loved, her, truly. Strike!—Electra,
My father has wanted vengeance longer.

THE PEOPLE BELOW   Orestes, Orestes!

ELECTRA (*pointing to* CASSANDRA)   Her
—your mother—she killed him.

ORESTES (*turning and striking*) How tall you have grown,
mother.

CASSANDRA (*falling*) I . . . waited long for it . . .

ORESTES
I have killed my mother and my mother—two mothers—see,
there they lie—I have gone home twice. You put it in
And the flesh yields to it . . . (*He goes down the stair.*)
Now, to find her again
All through the forest . . .

ELECTRA   Let him pass, Mycenæans. Avoid
his sword. Let him pass, pass. The madness of the
house
Perches on him.

A LEADER OF THE MYCENÆANS   Daughter of Agamemnon,
You with constancy and force
In the issueless thing have found an issue. Now it is for
us the kingless city
To find a ruler. Rest in the house. As for the young man,
Though he has done justice, and no hand in Mycenæ is
raised against him, for him there is no issue.
We let him go on; and if he does not slay himself with the
red sword he will die in the mountain.
With us be peace. Rest in the house, daughter of Agamem-
non. The old madness, with your brother,

Go out of our gates.

ELECTRA   A house to rest in! . . . Gather up the
dead: I will go in; I have learned strength.

III

They carried the dead down the great stair; the slaves with
pails of water and sand scoured the dark stains.
The people meeting in another place to settle the troubled
city the stair was left vacant,
The porch untrampled, and about twilight one of the great
stones: The world is younger than we are,
Yet now drawing to an end, now that the seasons falter.
Then another, that had been spared the blood-bath:
What way do they falter?—There fell warm rain, the first
answered, in the midst of summer. A little afterward
Cold rain came down; and sand was rubbed over me as
when the winds blow. This in the midst of summer.
—I did not feel it, said the second sleepily. And a third:
The noisy and very mobile creatures
Will be quieted long before the world's end.—What creatures?
—The active ones, that have two ends let downward,
A mongrel race, mixed of soft stone with fugitive water.
The night deepened, the dull old stones
Droned at each other, the summer stars wheeled over above
them. Before dawn the son of Agamemnon
Came to the stair-foot in the darkness.

ORESTES   O stones of the house:
I entreat hardness: I did not live with you
Long enough in my youth. . . . I will go up to where I killed
her. . . . We must face things down, mother,
Or they'd devour us. . . . Nobody? . . . Even the stones
have been scrubbed. A keen housekeeper, sweet Electra.
. . . It would be childish to forget it; the woman has cer-
tainly been killed, and I think it was I
Her son did it. Something not done before in the world.
Here is the penalty:

[72]

You gather up all your forces to the act, and afterward
Silence, no voice, no ghost, vacancy, but all's not expended.
   Those powers want bitter action. No object.
Deeds are too easy. Our victims are too fragile, they ought
   to have thousands of lives, you strike out once only
The sky breaks like a bubble. . . . No, wife of Ægisthus,—
   why should I mask it?—mother, my mother,
The one soft fiber that went mad yesterday's
Burnt out of me now, there is nothing you could touch if you
   should come; but you have no power, you dead
Are a weak people. This is the very spot: I was here, she
   here: and I walk over it not trembling,
Over the scrubbed stones to the door. (*He knocks with the
   sword-hilt.*) They sleep well. But my sister having all
   her desire
Better than any. (*He knocks again.*)
THE PORTER (*through the door*) Who is there?
ORESTES The owner of the house. Orestes.
THE PORTER Go away, drunkard.
ORESTES Shall I tell my servants to break in the door and
   whip the porter?
THE PORTER Oh, Oh! You men from Phocis, stand by me
   while I speak to the door. (*Having opened the door,
   holding a torch.*) Is it you truly, my lord? We thought,
   we thought . . . we pray you to enter the house, my lord
   Orestes.
ORESTES You are to waken my sister.
I'll speak with her here.
ELECTRA (*at the door*) Oh! You are safe, you are well!
   Did you think I could be sleeping? But it is true,
I have slept soundly. Come, come.
ORESTES   A fellow in the forest
Told me you'd had the stone scrubbed . . . I mean, that
   you'd entered the house, received as Agamemnon's
   daughter
In the honor of the city. So I free to go traveling have come
   with—what's the word, Electra?—farewell.

[78]

Have come to bid you farewell.

ELECTRA   It means—you are going
somewhere? Come into the house, Orestes, tell me . . .

ORESTES
The cape's rounded. I have not shipwrecked.

ELECTRA   Around the
rock we have passed safely is the hall of this house,
The throne in the hall, the shining lordship of Mycenæ.

ORESTES   No:
the open world, the sea and its wonders.
You thought the oars raked the headland in the great storm
   —what, for Mycenæ?

ELECTRA   Not meanest of the Greek cities:
Whose king captained the world into Asia. Have you sud-
   denly become . . . a God, brother, to over-vault
Agamemnon's royalty? O come in, come in. I am cold, cold.
   I pray you.

ORESTES   Fetch a cloak, porter.
If I have outgrown the city a little—I have earned it. Did
   you notice, Electra, she caught at the sword
As the point entered: the palm of her right hand was slashed
   to the bone before the mercy of the point
Slept in her breast: the laid-open palm it was that under-
   mined me . . . Oh, the cloak. It's a blond night,
We'll walk on the stones: no chill, the stars are mellow. If
   I dare remember
Yesterday . . . because I have conquered, the soft fiber's
   burnt out.

ELECTRA   You have conquered: possess: enter the house,
Take up the royalty.

ORESTES   You were in my vision to-night in the
   forest, Electra, I thought I embraced you
More than brotherwise . . . possessed, you call it . . . en-
   tered the fountain—

ELECTRA   Oh, hush. *Therefore* you would not
   kill her!

ORESTES

I killed. It is foolish to darken things with words. I was
   here, she there, screaming. Who if not I?

ELECTRA

The hidden reason: the bitter kernel of your mind that has
   made you mad: I that learned strength
Yesterday, I have no fear.

ORESTES   Fear? The city is friendly and
   took you home with honor, they'll pay
Phocis his wage, you will be quiet.

ELECTRA   Are you resolved to under-
   stand nothing, Orestes?
I am not Agamemnon, only his daughter. You are Agamem-
   non. Beggars and the sons of beggars
May wander at will over the world, but Agamemnon has his
   honor and high Mycenæ
Is not to be cast.

ORESTES   Mycenæ for a ship: who will buy kingdom
And sell me a ship with oars?

ELECTRA   Dear: listen. Come to the
   parapet where it hangs over the night:
The ears at the door hinder me. Now, let the arrow-eyed
   stars hear, the night, not men, as for the Gods
No one can know them, whether they be angry or pleased,
   tall and terrible, standing apart,
When they make signs out of the darkness. . . . I cannot tell
   you. . . . You will stay here, brother?

ORESTES   I'll go
To the edge and over it. Sweet sister, if you've got a mes-
   sage for them, the dark ones?

ELECTRA   You do not mean
Death; but a wandering; what does it matter what you mean?
   I know two ways and one will quiet you.
You shall choose either.

ORESTES   But I am quiet. It is more regular than
   a sleeping child's: be untroubled,
Yours burns, it is you trembling.

[75]

ELECTRA   Should I not tremble? It is
  only a little to offer,
But all that I have.
ORESTES   Offer?
ELECTRA   It is accomplished: my father is
  avenged: the fates and the body of Electra
Are nothing. But for Agamemnon to rule in Mycenæ: that is
  not nothing. O my brother
You are Agamemnon: rule: take all you will: nothing is de-
  nied you. The Gods have redressed evil
And clamped the balance.
ORESTES   No doubt they have done what they desired.
ELECTRA   And yours,
  yours? I will not suffer her
Justly punished to dog you over the end of the world. Your
  desire? Speak it openly, Orestes.
She is to be conquered: if her ghost were present on the
  stones—let it hear you. I will make war on her
With my life, or with my body.
ORESTES   What strange martyrdom, Electra,
  what madness for sacrifice
Makes your eyes burn like two fires on a watch-tower, though
  the night darkens?
ELECTRA   What you want you shall have:
And rule in Mycenæ. Nothing, nothing is denied you. If I
  knew which of the two choices
Would quiet you, I would do and not speak, not ask you.
  Tell me, tell me. Must I bear all the burden,
I weaker, and a woman? You and I were two hawks quar-
  tering the field for living flesh Orestes
Under the storm of the memory
Of Agamemnon: we struck: we tore the prey, that dog and
  that woman. Suddenly since yesterday
You have shot up over me and left me,
You are Agamemnon, you are the storm of the living pres-
  ence, the very King, and I, lost wings
Under the storm, would die for you. . . . You do not speak

[76]

yet? . . . Mine to say it all? . . . You know me a maiden,
   Orestes,
You have always been with me, no man has even touched my
   cheek. It is not easy for one unmarried
And chaste, to name both choices. The first is easy. That
   terrible dream in the forest: if fear of desire
Drives you away: it is easy for me not to be. I never have
   known
Sweetness in life: all my young days were given—

ORESTES   I thought
   to be silent was better,
And understand you: afterwards I'll speak.

ELECTRA   —to the noise of
   blood crying for blood, a crime to be punished,
A house to be emptied: these things are done: and now I am
   lonely, and what becomes of me is not important.
There's water, and there are points and edges, pain's only a
   moment: I'd do it and not speak, but nobody knows
Whether it would give you peace or madden you again, I'd
   not be leagued with that bad woman against you,
And these great walls sit by the crater, terrible desires blow
   through them. O brother I'll never blame you,
I share the motherhood and the fatherhood, I can conceive the
   madness, if you desire too near
The fountain: tell me: I also love you: not that way, but
   enough to suffer. What needs to be done
To make peace for you, tell me. I shall so gladly die to
   make it for you: or so gladly yield you
What you know is maiden. You are the King; have all your
   will: only remain in steep Mycenæ,
In the honor of our father. Not yet: do not speak yet. You
   have said it is not
Remorse drives you away: monsters require monsters, to have
   let her live a moment longer
Would have been the crime: therefore it cannot be but desire
   drives you: or the fear of desire: dearest,

It is known horror unlocks the heart, a shower of things hid-
    den: if that which happened yesterday unmasked
A beautiful brother's love and showed more awful eyes in it:
    all that our Gods require is courage.
Let me see the face, let the eyes pierce me. What, dearest?
    Here in the stiff cloth of the sacred darkness
Fold over fold hidden, above the sleeping city,
By the great stones of the door, under the little golden fal-
    cons that swarm before dawn up yonder,
In the silence . . . must I dare to woo you,
I whom man never wooed? to let my hand glide under the
    cloak. . . . O you will stay! these arms
Making so soft and white a bond around you . . . I also
    begin to love—that way, Orestes,
Feeling the hot hard flesh move under the loose cloth, shud-
    der against me. . . . Ah, your mouth, Ah,
The burning—kiss me—

ORESTES   We shall never ascend this mountain.
    So it might come true: we have to be tough against them,
Our dreams and visions, or they true themselves into flesh. It
    is sweet: I faint for it: the old stones here
Have seen more and not moved. A custom of the house. To
    accept you, little Electra, and go my journey
To-morrow: you'd call cheating. Therefore: we shall not
    go up this mountain dearest, dearest,
To-night nor ever. It's Clytemnestra in you. But the dead
    are a weak tribe. If I had Agamemnon's
We'd live happily sister and lord it in Mycenæ—be a king
    like the others—royalty and incest
Run both in the stream of the blood. Who scrubbed the
    stones there?

ELECTRA   Slaves. O fire burn me! Enter and lay
    waste,
Deflower, trample, break down, pillage the little city,
Make what breach you will, with flesh or a spear, give it to
    the spoiler. See, as I tear the garment.

What if I called it cheating?   Be cruel and treacherous: I'll
   run my chances
On the bitter mercies of to-morrow.

ORESTES   Bitter they would be.   No.

ELECTRA   It's clear
   that for this reason
You'd sneak out of Mycenæ and be lost outward.   Taste first,
   bite the apple, once dared and tried
Desire will be not terrible.   It's doglike to run off whining.
   Remember it was I that urged
Yesterday's triumph.   You: life was enough: let them live.
   I drove on, burning; your mind, reluctant metal,
I dipped it in fire and forged it sharp, day after day I beat
   and burned against you, and forged
A sword: I the arm.   Are you sorry it's done?   Now again
   with hammer and burning heat I beat against you,
You will not be sorry.   We two of all the world, we alone,
Are fit for each other, we have so wrought . . . O eyes
   scorning the world, storm-feathered hawk my hands
Caught out of the air and made you a king over this rock, O
   axe with the gold helve, O star
Alone over the storm, beacon to men over blown seas, you will
   not flee fate, you will take
What the Gods give.   What is a man not ruling?   An ant in
   the hill: ruler or slave the choice is,
—Or a runaway slave, your pilgrim portion, buffeted over the
   borders of the lands, publicly
Whipped in the cities.   But you, you will bind the north-star
   on your forehead, you will stand up in Mycenæ
Stone, and a king.

ORESTES   I am stone enough not to be changed by
   words, nor by the sweet and burning flame of you,
Beautiful Electra.

ELECTRA   Well then: we've wasted our night.   See,
   there's the morning star
I might have draggled into a metaphor of you.   A fool: a
   boy: no king.

[79]

ORESTES   It would have been better
To have parted kindlier, for it is likely
We shall have no future meeting.
ELECTRA   You will let this crime (the
     God commanded) that dirtied the old stones here
Make division forever?
ORESTES   Not the crime, the wakening. That
     deed is past, it is finished, things past
Make no division afterward, they have no power, they have
     become nothing at all: this much
I have learned at a crime's knees.
ELECTRA   Yet we are divided.
ORESTES   Because I have
     suddenly awakened, I will not waste inward
Upon humanity, having found a fairer object.
ELECTRA   Some nymph of
     the field? I knew this coldness
Had a sick root: a girl in the north told me about the hill-
     shepherds who living in solitude
Turn beast with the ewes, their oreads baa to them through
     the matted fleece and they run mad, what madness
Met you in the night and sticks to you?
ORESTES   I left the madness of
     the house, to-night in the dark, with you it walks yet.
How shall I tell you what I have learned? Your mind is like
     a hawk's or like a lion's, this knowledge
Is out of the order of your mind, a stranger language. To
     wild beasts and the blood of kings
A verse blind in the book.
ELECTRA   At least my eyes can see dawn gray-
     ing: tell and not mock me, our moment
Dies in a moment.
ORESTES   Here is the last labor
To spend on humanity. I saw a vision of us move in the
     dark: all that we did or dreamed of
Regarded each other, the man pursued the woman, the woman
     clung to the man, warriors and kings

[80]

Strained at each other in the darkness, all loved or fought
    inward, each one of the lost people
Sought the eyes of another that another should praise him;
    sought never his own but another's; the net of desire
Had every nerve drawn to the center, so that they writhed
    like a full draught of fishes, all matted
In the one mesh; when they look backward they see only a
    man standing at the beginning,
Or forward, a man at the end; or if upward, men in the
    shining bitter sky striding and feasting,
Whom you call Gods . . .
It is all turned inward, all your desires incestuous, the woman
    the serpent, the man the rose-red cavern,
Both human, worship forever . . .

ELECTRA   You have dreamed wretchedly.

ORESTES   I have
    seen the dreams of the people and not dreamed them.
As for me, I have slain my mother.

ELECTRA   No more?

ORESTES   And the gate's
    open, the gray boils over the mountain, I have greater
Kindred than dwell under a roof. Didn't I say this would
    be dark to you? I have cut the meshes
And fly like a freed falcon. To-night, lying on the hillside,
    sick with those visions, I remembered
The knife in the stalk of my humanity; I drew and it broke;
    I entered the life of the brown forest
And the great life of the ancient peaks, the patience of stone,
    I felt the changes in the veins
In the throat of the mountain, a grain in many centuries, we
    have our own time, not yours; and I was the stream
Draining the mountain wood; and I the stag drinking; and
    I was the stars,
Boiling with light, wandering alone, each one the lord of his
    own summit; and I was the darkness
Outside the stars, I included them, they were a part of me.
    I was mankind also, a moving lichen

[81]

On the cheek of the round stone . . . they have not made
    words for it, to go behind things, beyond hours and ages,
And be all things in all time, in their returns and passages, in
    the motionless and timeless center,
In the white of the fire . . . how can I express the excellence
    I have found, that has no color but clearness;
No honey but ecstasy; nothing wrought nor remembered;
    no undertone nor silver second murmur
That rings in love's voice, I and my loved are one; no desire
    but fulfilled; no passion but peace,
The pure flame and the white, fierier than any passion; no
    time but spheral eternity: Electra,
Was that your name before this life dawned—

ELECTRA   Here is mere
    death.   Death like a triumph I'd have paid to keep you
A king in high Mycenæ: but here is shameful death, to die
    because I have lost you.   They'll say
Having done justice Agamemnon's son ran mad and was lost
    in the mountain; but Agamemnon's daughter
Hanged herself from a beam of the house: O bountiful hands
    of justice!   This horror draws upon me
Like stone walking.

ORESTES   What fills men's mouths is nothing; and
    your threat is nothing; I have fallen in love outward.
If I believed you—it is I that am like stone walking.

ELECTRA   I can endure
    even to hate you,
But that's no matter.   Strength's good.   You are lost.   I here
    remember the honor of the house, and Agamemnon's.

She turned and entered the ancient house.   Orestes walked in
    the clear dawn; men say that a serpent
Killed him in high Arcadia.   But young or old, few years or
    many, signified less than nothing
To him who had climbed the tower beyond time, consciously,
    and cast humanity, entered the earlier fountain.

[82]

NIGHT

The ebb slips from the rock, the sunken
Tide-rocks lift streaming shoulders
Out of the slack, the slow west
Sombering its torch; a ship's light
Shows faintly, far out,
Over the weight of the prone ocean
On the low cloud.

Over the dark mountain, over the dark pinewood,
Down the long dark valley along the shrunken river,
Returns the splendor without rays, the shining of shadow,
Peace-bringer, the matrix of all shining and quieter of shining.
Where the shore widens on the bay she opens dark wings
And the ocean accepts her glory. O soul worshipful of her
You like the ocean have grave depths where she dwells always,
And the film of waves above that takes the sun takes also
Her, with more love. The sun-lovers have a blond favorite,
A father of lights and noises, wars, weeping and laughter,
Hot labor, lust and delight and the other blemishes.
    Quietness
Flows from her deeper fountain; and he will die; and she is
    immortal.

Far off from here the slender
Flocks of the mountain forest
Move among stems like towers
Of the old redwoods to the stream,
No twig crackling; dip shy
Wild muzzles into the mountain water
Among the dark ferns.

O passionately at peace you being secure will pardon
The blasphemies of glowworms, the lamp in my tower, the
    fretfulness
Of cities, the crescents of the planets, the pride of the stars.
This August night in a rift of cloud Antares reddens,
The great one, the ancient torch, a lord among lost children,
The earth's orbit doubled would not girdle his greatness,
    one fire
Globed, out of grasp of the mind enormous; but to you
    O Night
What? Not a spark? What flicker of a spark in the faint
    far glimmer
Of a lost fire dying in the desert, dim coals of a sand-pit the
    Bedouins
Wandered from at dawn . . . Ah singing prayer to what
    gulfs tempted
Suddenly are you more lost? To us the near-hand mountain
Be a measure of height, the tide-worn cliff at the sea-gate a
    measure of continuance.

The tide, moving the night's
Vastness with lonely voices,
Turns, the deep dark-shining
Pacific leans on the land,
Feeling his cold strength
To the outmost margins: you Night will resume
The stars in your time.

O passionately at peace when will that tide draw shoreward?
Truly the spouting fountains of light, Antares, Arcturus,
Tire of their flow, they sing one song but they think silence.
The striding winter giant Orion shines, and dreams darkness.
And life, the flicker of men and moths and the wolf on the hill,
Though furious for continuance, passionately feeding, passionately
    passionately
Remaking itself upon its mates, remembers deep inward
The calm mother, the quietness of the womb and the egg,

The primal and the latter silences: dear Night it is memory
Prophesies, prophecy that remembers, the charm of the dark.
And I and my people, we are willing to love the four-score
  years
Heartily; but as a sailor loves the sea, when the helm is for
  harbor.

Have men's minds changed,
Or the rock hidden in the deep of the waters of the soul
Broken the surface? A few centuries
Gone by, was none dared not to people
The darkness beyond the stars with harps and habitations.
But now, dear is the truth. Life is grown sweeter and
  lonelier,
And death is no evil.

BIRDS

The fierce musical cries of a couple of sparrowhawks hunting
    on the headland,
Hovering and darting, their heads northwestward,
Prick like silver arrows shot through a curtain the noise of
    the ocean
Trampling its granite; their red backs gleam
Under my window around the stone corners; nothing
    gracefuller, nothing
Nimbler in the wind. Westward the wave-gleaners,
The old gray sea-going gulls are gathered together, the north-
    west wind wakening
Their wings to the wild spirals of the wind-dance.
Fresh as the air, salt as the foam, play birds in the bright
    wind, fly falcons
Forgetting the oak and the pinewood, come gulls
From the Carmel sands and the sands at the river-mouth,
    from Lobos and out of the limitless
Power of the mass of the sea, for a poem
Needs multitude, multitudes of thoughts, all fierce, all flesh-
    eaters, musically clamorous
Bright hawks that hover and dart headlong, and ungainly
Gray hungers fledged with desire of transgression, salt slimed
    beaks, from the sharp
Rock-shores of the world and the secret waters.

FOG

Invisible gulls with human voices cry in the sea-cloud
"There is room, wild minds,
Up high in the cloud; the web and the feather remember
Three elements, but here
Is but one, and the webs and the feathers
Subduing but the one
Are the greater, with strength and to spare." You dream,
   wild criers,
The peace that all life
Dreams gluttonously, the infinite self that has eaten
Environment, and lives
Alone, unencroached on, perfectly gorged, one God.
Cæsar and Napoleon
Visibly acting their dream of that solitude, Christ and
   Gautama,
Being God, devouring
The world with atonement for God's sake . . . ah sacred
   hungers,
The conqueror's, the prophet's,
The lover's, the hunger of the sea-beaks, slaves of the last
   peace,
Worshippers of oneness.

BOATS IN A FOG

Sports and gallantries, the stage, the arts, the antics of
    dancers,
The exuberant voices of music,
Have charm for children but lack nobility; it is bitter
    earnestness
That makes beauty; the mind
Knows, grown adult.
            A sudden fog-drift muffled the ocean,
A throbbing of engines moved in it,
At length, a stone's throw out, between the rocks and the
    vapor,
One by one moved shadows
Out of the mystery, shadows, fishing-boats, trailing each other,
Following the cliff for guidance,
Holding a difficult path between the peril of the sea-fog
And the foam on the shore granite.
One by one, trailing their leader, six crept by me,
Out of the vapor and into it,
The throb of their engines subdued by the fog, patient and
    cautious,
Coasting all round the peninsula
Back to the buoys in Monterey harbor. A flight of pelicans
Is nothing lovelier to look at;
The flight of the planets is nothing nobler; all the arts lose
    virtue
Against the essential reality
Of creatures going about their business among the equally
Earnest elements of nature.

GRANITE AND CYPRESS

White-maned, wide-throated, the heavy-shouldered children of
    the wind leap at the sea-cliff.
The invisible falcon
Brooded on water and bred them in wide waste places, in a
    bride-chamber wide to the stars' eyes
In the center of the ocean,
Where no prows pass nor island is lifted . . . the sea beyond
    Lobos is whitened with the falcon's
Passage, he is here now,
The sky is one cloud, his wing-feathers hiss in the white grass,
    my sapling cypresses writhing
In the fury of his passage
Dare not dream of their centuries of future endurance of
    tempest.   (I have granite and cypress,
Both long-lasting,
Planted in the earth; but the granite sea-bowlders are prey
    to no hawk's wing, they have taken worse pounding,
Like me they remember
Old wars and are quiet; for we think that the future is one
    piece with the past, we wonder why tree-tops
And people are so shaken.)

VICES

Spirited people make a thousand jewels in verse and prose,
  and the restlessness of talent
Runs over and floods the stage or spreads its fever on canvas.
They are skilled in music too, the demon is never satisfied,
  they take to puppets, they invent
New arts, they take to drugs . . . and we all applaud our
  vices.
Mine, coldness and the tenor of a stone tranquillity; slow
  life, the growth of trees and verse,
Content the unagitable and somewhat earthfast nature.

PHENOMENA

Great-enough both accepts and subdues; the great frame takes
  all creatures;
From the greatness of their element they all take beauty.
Gulls; and the dingy freightship lurching south in the eye
  of a rain-wind;
The air-plane dipping over the hill; hawks hovering
The white grass of the headland; cormorants roosting upon
  the guano-
Whitened skerries; pelicans awind; sea-slime
Shining at night in the wave-stir like drowned men's lanterns;
  smugglers signaling
A cargo to land; or the old Point Pinos lighthouse
Lawfully winking over dark water; the flight of the twilight
  herons,
Lonely wings and a cry; or with motor-vibrations
That hum in the rock like a new storm-tone of the ocean's
  to turn eyes westward
The navy's new-bought Zeppelin going by in the twilight,
Far out seaward; relative only to the evening star and the
  ocean
It slides into a cloud over Point Lobos.

PEOPLE AND A HERON

A desert of weed and water-darkened stone under my western
   windows
The ebb lasted all afternoon,
And many pieces of humanity, men, women, and children,
   gathering shellfish,
Swarmed with voices of gulls the sea-breach.
At twilight they went off together, the verge was left vacant,
   an evening heron
Bent broad wings over the black ebb,
And left me wondering why a lone bird was dearer to me than
   many people.
Well: rare is dear: but also I suppose
Well reconciled with the world but not with our own natures
   we grudge to see them
Reflected on the world for a mirror.

HAUNTED COUNTRY

Here the human past is dim and feeble and alien to us
Our ghosts draw from the crowded future.
Fixed as the past how could it fail to drop weird shadows
And make strange murmurs about twilight?
In the dawn twilight metal falcons flew over the mountain,
Multitudes, and faded in the air; at moonrise
The farmer's girl by the still river is afraid of phantoms,
Hearing the pulse of a great city
Move on the water-meadow and stream off south; the country's
Children for all their innocent minds
Hide dry and bitter lights in the eye, they dream without
    knowing it
The inhuman years to be accomplished,
The inhuman powers, the servile cunning under pressure,
In a land grown old, heavy and crowded.
There are happy places that fate skips; here is not one of
    them;
The tides of the brute womb, the excess
And weight of life spilled out like water, the last migration
Gathering against this holier valley-mouth
That knows its fate beforehand, the flow of the womb,
    banked back
By the older flood of the ocean, to swallow it.

AUTUMN EVENING

Though the little clouds ran southward still, the quiet autumnal
Cool of the late September evening
Seemed promising rain, rain, the change of the year, the angel
Of the sad forest. A heron flew over
With that remote ridiculous cry, "Quawk," the cry
That seems to make silence more silent. A dozen
Flops of the wing, a drooping glide, at the end of the glide
The cry, and a dozen flops of the wing.
I watched him pass on the autumn-colored sky; beyond him
Jupiter shone for evening star.
The sea's voice worked into my mood, I thought "No matter
What happens to men . . . the world's well made though."

SHINE, PERISHING REPUBLIC

While this America settles in the mould of its vulgarity,
    heavily thickening to empire,
And protest, only a bubble in the molten mass, pops and
    sighs out, and the mass hardens,

I sadly smiling remember that the flower fades to make fruit,
    the fruit rots to make earth.
Out of the mother; and through the spring exultances,
    ripeness and decadence; and home to the mother.

You making haste haste on decay: not blameworthy; life is
    good, be it stubbornly long or suddenly
A mortal splendor: meteors are not needed less than
    mountains: shine, perishing republic.

But for my children, I would have them keep their distance
    from the thickening center; corruption
Never has been compulsory, when the cities lie at the
    monster's feet there are left the mountains.

And boys, be in nothing so moderate as in love of man, a
    clever servant, insufferable master.
There is the trap that catches noblest spirits, that caught—
    they say—God, when he walked on earth.

THE TREASURE

Mountains, a moment's earth-waves rising and hollowing;
 the earth too's an ephemerid; the stars——
Short-lived as grass the stars quicken in the nebula and dry
 in their summer, they spiral
Blind up space, scattered black seeds of a future; nothing
 lives long, the whole sky's
Recurrences tick the seconds of the hours of the ages of the
 gulf before birth, and the gulf
After death is like dated: to labor eighty years in a notch
 of eternity is nothing too tiresome,
Enormous repose after, enormous repose before, the flash of
 activity.
Surely you never have dreamed the incredible depths were
 prologue and epilogue merely
To the surface play in the sun, the instant of life, what is
 called life? I fancy
That silence is the thing, this noise a found word for it;
 interjection, a jump of the breath at that silence;
Stars burn, grass grows, men breathe: as a man finding
 treasure says "Ah!" but the treasure's the essence;
Before the man spoke it was there, and after he has spoken
 he gathers it, inexhaustible treasure.

JOY

Though joy is better than sorrow joy is not great;
Peace is great, strength is great.
Not for joy the stars burn, not for joy the vulture
Spreads her gray sails on the air
Over the mountain; not for joy the worn mountain
Stands, while years like water
Trench his long sides. "I am neither mountain nor bird
Nor star; and I seek joy."
The weakness of your breed: yet at length quietness
Will cover those wistful eyes.

PRACTICAL PEOPLE

Practical people, I have been told,
Weary of the sea for his waves go up and down
Endlessly to no visible purpose;
Tire of the tides, for the tides are tireless, the tides
Are well content with their own march-tune
And nothing accomplished is no matter to them.
It seems wasteful to practical people.
And that the nations labor and gather and dissolve
Into destruction; the stars sharpen
Their spirit of splendor, and then it dims, and the stars
Darken; and that the spirit of man
Sharpens up to maturity and cools dull
With age, dies, and rusts out of service;
And all these tidal gatherings, growth and decay,
Shining and darkening, are forever
Renewed; and the whole cycle impenitently
Revolves, and all the past is future:——
Make it a difficult world . . . for practical people.

WOODROW WILSON
(February, 1924.)

It said "Come home, here is an end, a goal,
Not the one raced for, is it not better indeed?   Victory you
    know requires
Force to sustain victory, the burden is never lightened, but
    final defeat
Buys peace: you have praised peace, peace without victory."

He said "It seems I am traveling no new way,
But leaving my great work unfinished how can I rest?   I
    enjoyed a vision,
Endured betrayal, you must not ask me to endure final defeat,
Visionless men, blind hearts, blind mouths, live still."

It said "Yet perhaps your vision was less great
Than some you scorned, it has not proved even so practicable;
    Lenine
Enters this pass with less reluctance.   As to betrayals: there
    are so many
Betrayals, the Russians and the Germans know."

He said "I knew I have enemies, I had not thought
To meet one at this brink: shall not the mocking voices die
    in the grave?"
It said "They shall.   Soon there is silence."   "I dreamed
    this end," he said, "when the prow
Of the long ship leaned against dawn, my people

Applauded me, and the world watched me. Again
I dreamed it at Versailles, the time I sent for the ship, and
    the obstinate foreheads
That shared with me the settlement of the world flinched
    at my threat and yielded.
That is all gone. . . . Do I remember this darkness?"

It said "No man forgets it but a moment.
The darkness before the mother, the depth of the return."
    "I thought," he answered,
"That I was drawn out of this depth to establish the earth
    on peace. My labor
Dies with me, why was I drawn out of this depth?"

It said "Loyal to your highest, sensitive, brave,
Sanguine, some few ways wise, you and all men are drawn
    out of this depth
Only to be these things you are, as flowers for color, falcons
    for swiftness,
Mountains for mass and quiet. Each for its quality

Is drawn out of this depth. Your tragic quality
Required the huge delusion of some major purpose to
    produce it.
What, that the God of the stars needed your help?" He said
    "This is my last
Worst pain, the bitter enlightenment that buys peace."

SCIENCE

Man, introverted man, having crossed
In passage and but a little with the nature of things this
    latter century
Has begot giants; but being taken up
Like a maniac with self-love and inward conflicts cannot
    manage his hybrids.
Being used to deal with edgeless dreams,
Now he's bred knives on nature turns them also inward: they
    have thirsty points though.
His mind forebodes his own destruction;
Actæon who saw the goddess naked among leaves and his
    hounds tore him.
A little knowledge, a pebble from the shingle,
A drop from the oceans: who would have dreamed this
    infinitely little too much?

THE TORCH-BEARERS' RACE

Here is the world's end. When our fathers forded the first
river in Asia we crossed the world's end;
And when the North Sea throbbed under their keels, the
world's end;
And when the Atlantic surge rolled English oak in the
sea-trough: always there was farther to go,
A new world piecing out the old one: but ours, our new world?
Dark and enormous rolls the surf; down on the mystical
tide-line under the cliffs at moonset
Dead tribes move, remembering the scent of their hills, the
lost hunters
Our fathers hunted; they driven westward died the sun's
death, they dread the depth and hang at the land's hem,
And are unavenged; frail ghosts, and ghostlike in their lives
too,
Having only a simple hunger for all our complication of
desires.   Dark and enormous
Rolls the surf of the far storms of the heart of the ocean;
The old granite breaks into white torches the heavy-shouldered
children of the wind . . . our ancient wanderings
West from the world's birth what sea-bound breaking shall
flame up torchlike?
I am building a thick stone pillar upon this shore, the very
turn of the world, the long migration's
End; the sun goes on but we have come up to an end.
We have climbed at length to a height, to an end, this end:
shall we go down again to Mother Asia?
Some of us will go down, some will abide, but we sought

More than to return to a mother. This huge, inhuman,
    remote, unruled, this ocean will show us
The inhuman road, the unruled attempt, the remote lode-star.
The torch-bearers' race: it is run in a dusk; when the
    emptied racer drops unseen at the end of his course
A fresh hand snatches the hilt of the light, the torch flies
    onward
Though the man die. Not a runner knows where the light
    was lighted, not a runner knows where it carries fire to,
Hand kisses hand in the dark, the torch passes, the man
Falls, and the torch passes. It gleamed across Euphrates
    mud, shone on Nile shore, it lightened
The little homely Ionian water and the sweet Ægean.
O perfect breathing of the runners, those narrow courses,
    names like the stars' names, Sappho, Alcæus,
And Æschylus a name like the first eagle's; but the torch
    westering
The seas widened, the earth's bloom hardened, the stone rose
    Rome seeding the earth, but the torch northering
Lightened the Atlantic . . . O flame, O beauty and shower
    of beauty,
There is yet one ocean and then no more, God whom you
    shine to walks there naked, on the final Pacific,
Not in a man's form.
                    The torch answered: Have I kindled a
    morning?
For again, this old world's end is the gate of a world fire-new,
    of your wild future, wild as a hawk's dream,
Ways hung on nothing, like stars, feet shaking earth off;
    that long way
Was a labor in a dream, will you wake now? The eaglets
    rustle in the aerie, the red eyes of dawn stabbing up
    through the nest-side,
You have walked in a dream, consumed with your fathers
    and your mothers, you have loved
Inside the four walls of humanity, passions turned inward,

incestuous desires and a fighting against ghosts, but the
    clarions
Of light have called morning.
                                What, not to be tangled any more in
    the blinding
Rays of reflected desire, the man with the woman, the woman
    with the child, the daughter with the father, but freed
Of the web self-woven, the burning and the blistering strands
    running inward?
Those rays to be lightened awide, to shine up the star-path,
    subduing the world outward? Oh chicks in the high
    nest be fledged now,
Having found out flight in the air to make wing to the
    height, fierce eye-flames
Of the eaglets be strengthened, to drink of the fountain of
    the beauty of the sun of the stars, and to gaze in his
    face, not a father's,
And motherless and terrible and here.
                                But I at the gate, I
    falling
On the gate-sill add this: When the ancient wisdom is
    folded like a wine-stained cloth and laid up in darkness.
And the old symbols forgotten, in the glory of that your
    hawk's dream
Remember that the life of mankind is like the life of a man,
    a flutter from darkness to darkness
Across the bright hair of a fire, so much of the ancient
Knowledge will not be annulled. What unimaginable op-
    ponent to end you?
                        There is one fountain
Of power, yours and that last opponent's, and of long peace.

TAMAR

I

A night the half-moon was like a dancing-girl,
No, like a drunkard's last half-dollar
Shoved on the polished bar of the eastern hill-range,
Young Cauldwell rode his pony along the sea-cliff;
When she stopped, spurred; when she trembled, drove
The teeth of the little jagged wheels so deep
They tasted blood; the mare with four slim hooves
On a foot of ground pivoted like a top,
Jumped from the crumble of sod, went down, caught, slipped;
Then, the quick frenzy finished, stiffening herself
Slid with her drunken rider down the ledges,
Shot from sheer rock and broke
Her life out on the rounded tidal boulders.

The night you know accepted with no show of emotion the
    little accident; grave Orion
Moved northwest from the naked shore, the moon moved to
    meridian, the slow pulse of the ocean
Beat, the slow tide came in across the slippery stones; it
    drowned the dead mare's muzzle and sluggishly
Felt for the rider; Cauldwell's sleepy soul came back from
    the blind course curious to know
What sea-cold fingers tapped the walls of its deserted ruin.
    Pain, pain and faintness, crushing
Weights, and a vain desire to vomit, and soon again
The icy fingers, they had crept over the loose hand and lay in
    the hair now. He rolled sidewise

[105]

Against mountains of weight and for another half-hour lay
    still. With a gush of liquid noises
The wave covered him head and all, his body
Crawled without consciousness and like a creature with no
    bones, a seaworm, lifted its face
Above the sea-wrack of a stone; then a white twilight grew
    about the moon, and above
The ancient water, the everlasting repetition of the dawn.
    You shipwrecked horseman
So many and still so many and now for you the last. But
    when it grew daylight
He grew quite conscious; broken ends of bone ground on
    each other among the working fibers
While by half-inches he was drawing himself out of the sea-
    wrack up to sandy granite,
Out of the tide's path. Where the thin ledge tailed into flat
    cliff he fell asleep. . . .
            Far seaward
The daylight moon hung like a slip of cloud against the
    horizon. The tide was ebbing
From the dead horse and the black belt of sea-growth.
    Cauldwell seemed to have felt her crying beside him,
His mother, who was dead. He thought "If I had a month
    or two of life yet
I would remember to be decent, only it's now too late, I'm
    finished, mother, mother,
I'm sorry." After that he thought only of pain and raging
    thirst until the sundown
Reddened the sea, and hands were reaching for him and
    drawing him up the cliff.

           His sister Tamar
Nursed him in the big westward bedroom
Of the old house on Point Lobos. After fever
A wonderful day of peace and pleasant weakness
Brought home to his heart the beauty of things. "O Tamar
I've thrown away years like rubbish. Listen, Tamar,

It would be better for me to be a cripple,
Sit on the steps and watch the forest grow up the hill
Or a new speck of moss on some old rock
That takes ten years agrowing, than waste
Shame and my spirit on Monterey rye whiskey,
And worse, and worse. I shan't be a cripple, Tamar.
We'll walk along the blessed old gray sea,
And up in the hills and watch the spring come home."

Youth is a troublesome but a magical thing,
There is little more to say for it when you've said
Young bones knit easily; he that fell in December
Walked in the February fields. His sister Tamar
Was with him, and his mind ran on her name,
But she was saying, "We laugh at poor Aunt Stella
With her spirit visitors: Lee, something told her truth.
Last August, you were hunting deer, you had been gone
Ten days or twelve, we heard her scream at night,
I went to the room, she told me
She'd seen you lying all bloody on the sea-beach
By a dead deer, its blood dabbling the black weeds of the
    ebb."
"I was up Tassajara way," he answered,
"Far from the sea." "We were glad when you rode home
Safe, with the two bucks on the packhorse. But listen,
She said she watched the stars flying over you
In her vision, Orion she said, and made me look
Out of her window southward, where I saw
The stars they call the Scorpion, the red bead
With the curling tail. "Then it will be in winter,"
She whispered to me, "Orion is winter." "Tamar, Tamar,
Winter is over, visions are over and vanished,
The fields are winking full of poppies,
In a week or two I'll fill your arms with shining irises."

The winter sun went under and all that night there came a
    roaring from the south; Lee Cauldwell

Lay awake and heard the tough old house creak all her
      timbers; he was miserably lonely and vacant,
He'd put away the boyish jets of wickedness, loves with dark
      eyes in Monterey back-streets, liquor
And all its fellowship, what was left to live for but the
      farm-work, rain would come and hinder?
He heard the cypress trees that seemed to scream in the
      wind, and felt the ocean pounding granite.
His father and Tamar's, the old man David Cauldwell, lay in
      the eastern chamber; when the storm
Wakened him from the heartless fugitive slumber of age he
      rose and made a light, and lighted
The lamp not cold yet; night and day were nearly equal to
      him, he had seen too many; he dressed
Slowly and opened his Bible. In the neighboring rooms he
      heard on one side Stella Moreland,
His dead wife's sister, quieting his own sister, the idiot Jinny
      Cauldwell, who laughed and chuckled
Often for half the night long, an old woman with a child's
      mind and mostly sleepless; in the other
Chamber Tamar was moaning, for it seemed that nightmare
Within the house answered to storm without.
To Tamar it seemed that she was walking by the seaside
With her dear brother, who said "Here's where I fell,
A bad girl that I knew in Monterey pushed me over the cliff,
You can see blood still on the boulders." Where he
      vanished to
She could not tell, nor why she was crying "Lee. No.
No dearest brother, dearest brother no." But she cried vainly,
Lee was not there to help her, a wild white horse
Came out of the wave and trampled her with his hooves,
The horror that she had dreaded through her dreaming
With mystical foreknowledge. When it wakened her,
She like her father heard old Jinny chuckling
And Stella sighing and soothing her, and the southwind
Raging around the gables of the house and through the forest
      of the cypresses.

[108]

"When it rains it will be quieter," Tamar thought. She slept
 again, all night not a drop fell.
Old Cauldwell from his window saw the cloudy light seep up
 the sky from the overhanging
Hilltops, the dawn was dammed behind the hills but over-
 flowed at last and ran down on the sea.

II

Lee Cauldwell rode across the roaring southwind to the
 winter pasture up in the hills.
A hundred times he wanted Tamar, to show her some new
 beauty of canyon wildflowers, water
Dashing its ferns, or oaktrees thrusting elbows at the wind,
 black-oaks smoldering with foliage
And the streaked beauty of white-oak trunks, and redwood
 glens; he rode up higher across the rainwind
And found his father's cattle in a quiet hollow among the hills,
 their horns to the wind,
Quietly grazing. He returned another way, from the head-
 land over Wildcat Canyon,
Saw the immense water possessing all the west and saw Point
 Lobos
Gemmed in it, and the barn-roofs and the house-roof
Like ships' keels in the cypress tops, and thought of Tamar.
Toward sundown he approached the house; Will Andrews
Was leaving it and young Cauldwell said, "Listen, Bill
 Andrews,
We've had gay times together and ridden at night.
I've quit it, I don't want my old friends to visit my sister.
Better keep off the place." "I will," said the other,
"When Tamar tells me to." "You think my bones
Aren't mended yet, better keep off." Lee Cauldwell
Rode by to the stable wondering why his lips
Twitched with such bitter anger; Tamar wondered
Why he went up-stairs without a word or smile
Of pleasure in her. The old man David Cauldwell,

When Lee had told him news of the herd and that Ramon
Seemed faithful, and the calves flourished, the old man
    answered:
"I hear that there's a dance at Notley's Landing Saturday.
    You'll be riding
Down the coast, Lee. Don't kill the horse, have a good
    time." "No, I've had all I want, I'm staying
At home now, evenings." "Don't do it; better dance your
    pony down the cliffs again than close
Young life into a little box; you've been too wild; now I'm
    worn out, but I remember
Hell's in the box." Lee answered nothing, his father's lamp
    of thought was hidden awhile in words,
An old man's words, like the dry evening moths that choke a
    candle. A space, and he was saying,
"Come summer we'll be mixed into the bloody squabble out
    there, and you'll be going headforemost
Unless you make your life so pleasant you'd rather live it.
    I mayn't be living
To see you home or hear you're killed." Lee, smiling at him,
"A soldier's what I won't be, father." That night
He dreamed himself a soldier, an aviator
Duelling with a German above a battle
That looked like waves, he fired his gun and mounted
In steady rhythm; he must have been winged, he suddenly
Plunged and went through the soft and deadly surface
Of the deep sea, wakening in terror.
He heard his old Aunt Jinny chuckling,
Aunt Stella sighing and soothing her, and the southwind
Raging around the gables of the house and through the forest
    of the cypresses.

III

They two had unbridled the horses
And tied them with long halters near the thicket
Under Mal Paso bridge and wandered east

Into the narrow cleft, they had climbed the summit
On the right and looked across the sea.
The steep path down, "What are we for?" said Tamar
   wearily, "to want and want and not dare know it."
"Because I dropped the faded irises," Lee answered, "you're
   unhappy. They were all withered, Tamar.
We have grown up in the same house." "The withered house
Of an old man and a withered woman and an idiot woman.
   No wonder if we go mad, no wonder."
They came to the hid stream and Tamar said, "Sweet, green
   and cool,
After the mad white April sun: you wouldn't mind, Lee?
Here where it makes a pool: you mustn't look; but you're my
   brother. And then
I will stand guard for you." The murmur and splash of
   water made his fever fiercer; something
Unfelt before kept his eyes seaward: why should he dread to
   see the round arm and clear throat
Flash from the hollow stream? He trembled, thinking "O
   we are beasts, a beast, what am I for?
Was the old man right, I must be drunk and a dancer and
   feed on the cheap pleasures, or it's dangerous?
Lovely and thoughtless, if she knew me how she'd loathe and
   avoid me. Her brother, brother. My sister.
Better the life with the bones, and all at once have broken."
   Meanwhile Tamar
Uneasily dipped her wrists, and crouching in the leaf-grown
   bank
Saw her breasts in the dark mirror, she trembled backward
From a long ripple and timidly wading entered
The quiet translucence to the thighs. White-shining
Slender and virgin pillar, desire in water
Unhidden and half reflected among the interbranching
   ripples,
Arched with alder, over-woven with willow.
Ah Tamar, stricken with strange fever and feeling
Her own desirableness, half-innocent Tamar

Thought, "If I saw a snake in the water he would come now
And kill the snake, he is keen and fearless but he fears
Me I believe." Was it the wild rock coast
Of her breeding, and the reckless wind
In the beaten trees and the gaunt booming crashes
Of breakers under the rocks, or rather the amplitude
And wing-subduing immense earth-ending water
That moves all the west taught her this freedom? Ah Tamar,
It was not good, not wise, not safe, not provident,
Not even, for custom creates nature, natural,
Though all other license were; and surely her face
Grew lean and whitened like a mask, the lips
Thinned their rose to a split thread, the little breasts
Erected sharp bright buds but the white belly
Shuddered, sucked in. The lips writhed and no voice
Formed, and again, and a faint cry. "Tamar?"
He answered, and she answered, "Nothing. A snake in the
    water
Frightened me." And again she called his name.
"What is it, Tamar?" "Nothing. It is cold in the water.
Come, Lee, I have hidden myself all but the head.
Bathe, if you mean to bathe, and keep me company.
I won't look till you're in." He came, trembling.
He unclothed himself in a green depth and dared not
Enter the pool, but stared at the drawn scars
Of the old wound on his leg. "Come, Lee, I'm freezing.
Come, I won't look." He saw the clear-skinned shoulders
And the hollow of her back, he drowned his body
In the watery floor under the cave of foliage,
And heard her sobbing. When she turned, the great blue eyes
Under the auburn hair, streamed. "Lee.
We have stopped being children; I would have drowned
    myself;
If you hadn't taught me swimming—long ago—long ago,
    Lee—
When we were children." "Tamar, what is it, what is it?"
"Only that I want . . . death. You lie if you think

[112]

Another thing." She slipped face down and lay
In the harmless water, the auburn hair trailed forward
Darkened like weeds, the double arc of the shoulders
Floated, and when he had dragged her to the bank both arms
Clung to him, the white body in a sobbing spasm
Clutched him, he could not disentangle the white desire,
So they were joined (like drowning folk brought back
By force to bitter life) painfully, without joy.
The spasm fulfilled, poor Tamar, like one drowned indeed, lay
    pale and quiet
And careless of her nakedness. He, gulfs opening
Between the shapes of his thought, desired to rise and leave
    her and was ashamed to.
He lay by her side, the cheek he kissed was cold like a smooth
    stone, the blue eyes were half open,
The bright smooth body seemed to have suffered pain, not
    love. One of her arms crushed both her breasts,
The other lay in the grass, the fingers clutching toward the
    roots of the soft grass. "Tamar,"
He whispered, then she breathed shudderingly and
    answered, "We have it, we have it. Now I know.
It was my fault. I never shall be ashamed again." He said,
    "What shall I do? Go away?
Kill myself, Tamar?" She contracted all her body and
    crouched in the long grass, shivering.
"It hurts, there is blood here, I am too cold to bathe myself
    again. O brother, brother,
Mine and twice mine. You knew already, a girl has got to
    learn. I love you, I chose my teacher.
Mine, it was my doing." She flung herself upon him, cold
    white and smooth, with sobbing kisses.
"I am so cold, dearest, dearest." The horses at the canyon
    mouth tugged at their halters,
Dug pits under the restless forehooves, shivered in the
    hill-wind
At sundown, were not ridden till dark, it was near midnight
They came to the old house.

IV

When Jinny Cauldwell slept, the old woman with a child's
    mind, then Stella Moreland
Invoked her childish-minded dead, or lying blank-eyed in the
    dark egged on her dreams to vision,
Suffering for lack of audience, tasting the ecstasy of vision.
    This was the vaporous portion
She endured her life in the strength of, in the sea-shaken
    loneliness, little loved, nursing an idiot,
Growing bitterly old among the wind-torn Lobos cypress
    trunks. (O torture of needled branches
Doubled and gnarled, never a moment of quiet, the northwind
    or the southwind or the northwest.
For up and down the coast they are tall and terrible horsemen
    on patrol, alternate giants
Guarding the granite and sand frontiers of the last ocean;
    but here at Lobos the winds are torturers,
The old trees endure them. They blew always thwart the
    old woman's dreams and sometimes by her bedside
Stood, the south in russety black, the north in white, but the
    northwest, wave-green, sea-brilliant,
Scaled like a fish. She had also the sun and moon and
    mightier presences in her visions.) Tamar
Entered the room toward morning and stood ghost-like among
    the old woman's ghosts. The rolled-up eyes,
Dull white, with little spindles of iris touching the upper
    lids, played back the girl's blown candle
Sightlessly, but the spirit of sight that the eyes are tools of
    and it made them, saw her. "Ah Helen,"
Cried out the entranced lips, "We thought you were tired of
    the wind, we thought you never came now.
My sister's husband lies in the next room, go waken him,
    show him your beauty, call him with kisses.
He is old and the spittle when he dreams runs into his
    beard, but he is your lover and your brother."

"I am not Helen," she said, "what Helen, what Helen?"
"Who was not the wife but the sister of her man,
Mine was his wife." "My mother?" "And now he is an
  old hulk battered ashore. Show him your beauty,
Strip for him, Helen, as when he made you a seaweed bed in
  the cave. What if the beard is slimy
And the eyes run, men are not always young and fresh like you
  dead women." But Tamar clutching
The plump hand on the coverlet scratched it with her nails,
  the old woman groaned but would not waken,
And Tamar held the candle flame against the hand, the
  soot striped it, then with a scream
The old woman awoke, sat up, and fell back rigid on the
  bed. Tamar found place for the candle
On a little table at the bedside, her freed hands could not
  awaken a second answer
In the flesh that now for all its fatness felt like a warmed
  stone. But the idiot waked and chuckled,
Waved both hands at the candle saying, "My little star, my
  little star, come little star."
And to these three old Cauldwell sighing with sleeplessness
Entered, not noticed, and he stood in the open door. Tamar
  was bending
Over the bed, loose hair like burnished metal
Concealed her face and sharply cut across one rounded
  shoulder
The thin night-dress had slipped from. The old man her
  father
Feared, for a ghost of law-contemptuous youth
Slid through the chilly vaults of the stiff arteries,
And he said, "What is it, Tamar?" "She was screaming in
  a dream,
I came to quiet her, now she has gone stiff like iron.
Who is this woman Helen she was dreaming about?"
"Helen? Helen?" he answered slowly and Tamar
Believed she saw the beard and the hands tremble.
"It's too cold for you, Tamar, go back to bed

And I'll take care of her. A common name for women."
Old Jinny clapped her hands, "Little star, little star,
Twinkle all night!" and the stiff form on the bed began
    to speak,
In a changed voice and from another mode of being
And spirit of thought: "I cannot think that you have
    forgotten.
I was walking on the far side of the moon,
Whence everything is seen but the earth, and never forgot.
This girl's desire drew me home, we also had wanted
Too near our blood,
And to tangle the interbranching net of generations
With a knot sideways. Desire's the arrow-sprayer
And shoots into the stars. Poor little Tamar
He gave you a luckless name in memory of me
And now he is old forgets mine." "You are that Helen,"
Said Tamar leaning over the fat shape
The quiet and fleshless voice seemed issuing from,
A sound of youth from the old puffed lips, "What Helen?
    This man's . . .
Sister, this body was saying?" "By as much more
As you are of your brother." "Why," laughed Tamar
    trembling,
"Hundreds of nasty children do it, and we
Nothing but children." Then the old man: "Lies, lies, lies.
No ghost, a lying old woman. Your Aunt Helen
Died white as snow. She died before your mother died.
Your mother and this old woman always hated her,
This liar, as they hated me. I was too hard a nature
To die of it. Lily and Stella." "It makes me nothing,
My darling sin a shadow and me a doll on wires,"
Thought Tamar with one half her spirit; and the other half
    said,
"Poor lies, words without meaning. Poor Aunt Stella,
The voices in her have no minds." "Poor little Tamar,"
Murmured the young voice from the swollen cavern,

"Though you are that woman's daughter, if we dead
Could be sorrowful for anyone but ourselves
I would be sorrowful for you, a trap so baited
Was laid to catch you when the world began,
Before the granite foundation. I too have tasted the sweet
    bait.
But you are the luckier, no one came home to me
To say there are no whips beyond death—but only memory,
And that can be endured." The room was quiet a moment,
And Tamar heard the wind moving out-doors. Then the
    idiot Jinny Cauldwell
Whose mind had been from birth a crippled bird but when
    she was twelve years old her mind's cage
Was covered utterly, like a bird-cage covered with its evening
    cloth when lamps are lighted,
And her memory skipped the more than forty years between
    but caught stray gleams of the sun of childhood,
She in her crumpled voice: "I'd rather play with Helen,
    go away Stella. Stella pinches me,
Lily laughs at me, Lily and Stella are not my sisters."
    "Jinny, Jinny,"
Said the old man shaking like a thin brick house-wall in an
    earthquake, "do you remember, Jinny?"
"Jinny don't like the old man," she answered, "give me the
    star, give me my star,"
She whined, stretching from bed to reach the candle, "why
    have they taken my little star?
Helen would give it to Jinny." Then Stella waking from the
    trance sighed and arose to quiet her
According to her night's habit. Tamar said, "You were
    screaming in your sleep." "I had great visions.
And I have forgotten them. There Jinny, there, there. It'll
    have the candle, will it? Pretty Jinny.
Will have candle to-morrow. Little Jinny let Aunt Stella
    sleep now." Old Cauldwell tottering
Went to his room; then Tamar said, "You were talking about
    his sister Helen, my aunt Helen,

[117]

You never told me about her." "She has been dead for forty
    years, what should we tell you about her?
Now little Jinny, pretty sister." And laying her hands upon
    the mattress of the bed
The old woman cradled it up and down, humming a weary
    song. Tamar stood vainly waiting
The sleep of the monstrous babe; at length because it would
    not sleep went to her room and heard it
Gurgle and whimper an hour; and the tired litanies of the
    lullabies; not quiet till daylight.

V

O swiftness of the swallow and strength
Of the stone shore, brave beauty of falcons,
Beauty of the blue heron that flies
Opposite the color of evening
From the Carmel River's reed-grown mouth
To her nest in the deep wood of the deer
Cliffs of peninsular granite engirdle,
O beauty of the fountains of the sun
I pray you enter a little chamber,
I have given you bodies, I have made you puppets,
I have made idols for God to enter
And tiny cells to hold your honey.
I have given you a dotard and an idiot,
An old woman puffed with vanity, youth but botched with
    incest,
O blower of music through the crooked bugles,
You that make signs of sins and choose the lame for angels,
Enter and possess. Being light you have chosen the dark
    lamps,
A hawk the sluggish bodies: therefore God you chose
Me; and therefore I have made you idols like these idols
To enter and possess.
                Tamar, finding no hope,
Slid back on passion, she had sought counsel of the dead

And found half-scornful pity and found her sin
Fore-dated; there was honey at least in shame
And secrecy in silence, and her lover
Could meet her afield or slip to her room at night
In serviceable safety. They learned, these two,
Not to look back nor forward; and but for the hint
Of vague and possible wreck every transgression
Paints on the storm-edge of the sky, their blue
Though it dulled a shade with custom shone serene
To the fifth moon, when the moon's mark on women
Died out of Tamar. She kept secret the warning,
How could she color such love with perplexed fear?
Her soul walked back and forth like a new prisoner
Feeling the plant of unescapable fate
Root in her body. There was death; who had entered water
To compass love might enter again to escape
Love's fruit; "But O, but O," she thought, "not to die now.
It is less than half a year
Since life turned sweet. If I knew one of the girls
My lover has known
She'd tell me what to do, how to be fruitless,
How to be . . . happy? They do it, they do it, all sin
Grew nothing to us that day in Mal Paso water.
A love sterile and sacred as the stars.
I will tell my lover, he will make me safe,
He will find means . . .
Sterile and sacred, and more than any woman
. . . Unhappy. Miserable," she sobbed, "miserable,
The rough and bitter water about the cliff's foot
Better to breathe."
                    When Lee was not by her side
She walked the cliffs to tempt them. The calm and large
Pacific surge heavy with summer rolling southeast from a far
     origin
Battered to foam among the stumps of granite below.
Tamar watched it swing up the little fjords and fountain
Not angrily in the blowholes; a gray vapor

Breathed up among the buttressed writhings of the cypress
trunks
And branches swollen with blood-red lichen. She went home
And her night was full of foolish dreams, two layers of dream,
unrelative in emotion
Or substance to the pain of her thoughts. One, the under-
current layer that seemed all night continuous,
Concerned the dead (and rather a vision than a dream, for
visions gathered on that house
Like corposant fire on the hoar mastheads of a ship wandering
strange waters), brown-skinned families
Came down the river and straggled through the wood to the
sea, they kindled fires by knobs of granite
And ate the sea-food that the plow still turns up rotting shells
of, not only around Point Lobos
But north and south wherever the earth breaks off to sea-rock;
Tamar saw the huddled bodies
Squat by the fires and sleep; but when the dawn came there
was throbbing music meant for daylight
And that weak people went where it led them and were noth-
ing; then Spaniards, priests and horseback soldiers,
Came down the river and wandered through the wood to the
sea, and hearing the universal music
Went where it led them and were nothing; and the English-
speakers
Came down the river and wandered through the wood to the
sea, among them Tamar saw her mother
Walking beside a nameless woman with no face nor breasts;
and the universal music
Led them away and they were nothing; but Tamar led her
father from that flood and saved him,
For someone named a church built on a rock, it was beautiful
and white, not fallen to ruin
Like the ruin by Carmel River; she led him to it and made
him enter the door, when he had entered
A new race came from the door and wandered down the river
to the sea and to Point Lobos.

This was the undertow of the dream, obscured by a brighter
    surface layer but seeming senseless.
The tides of the sea were quiet and someone said "because the
    moon is lost." Tamar looked up
And the moon dwindled, rocketing off through lonely space,
    and the people in the moon would perish
Of cold or of a star's fire: then Will Andrews curiously
    wounded in the face came saying
"Tamar, don't cry. What do you care? I will take care of
    you." Wakening, Tamar thought about him
And how he had stopped coming to see her. Perhaps it was
    another man came through her dream,
The wound in the face disguised him, but that morning Lee
    having ridden to Mill Creek
To bargain about some fields of winter pasture
Now that the advancing year withered the hill-grass,
Tamar went down and saddled her own pony,
A four-year-old, as white as foam, and cantered
Past San Jose creek-mouth and the Carrows' farm
(Where David Carrow and his fanatical blue eyes,
That afterward saw Christ on the hill, smiled at her passing)
And three miles up the Carmel Valley came
To the Andrews place where the orchards ran to the river
And all the air was rich with ripening apples.
She would not go to the house; she did not find
Whom she was seeking; at length sadly she turned
Homeward, for Lee might be home within two hours,
And on the Carmel bridge above the water
(Shrunken with summer and shot with water lichen,
The surface scaled with minute scarlet leaves,
The borders green with slimy threads) met whom she sought.
"Tamar," he said, "I've been to see you." "You hadn't
For a long time." "I had some trouble with Lee,
I thought you didn't want me." While they talked
Her eyes tasted his face: was it endurable?
Though it lacked the curious gash her dream had given
    him. . . .

"I didn't want you, you thought?"   "Lee said so."   "You
    might have waited
Till Tamar said so."   "Well," he answered, "I've been,
And neither of you was home but now I've met you."
—Well-looking enough; freckles, light hair, light eyes;
Not tall, but with a chest and hard wide shoulders,
And sitting the horse well—"O I can do it, I can do it,
Help me, God," murmured Tamar in her mind,
"How else—what else can I do?" and said, "Luck, isn't it?
What did you want to see me about?"   "I wanted . . .
Because I . . . like you, Tamar."—"Why should I be care-
    ful,"
She thought, "if I frighten him off what does it matter,
I have got a little beyond caring."   "Let's go down
Into the willow," she said, "we needn't be seen
Talking and someone tell him and make trouble
Here on the bridge."   They went to the hidden bank
Under the deep green willows, colored water
Stagnated on its moss up to the stems,
Coarse herbage hid the stirrups, Tamar slid from the saddle
As quietly as the long unwhitening wave
Moulds a sunk rock, and while he tethered the horses,
"I have been lonely," she said.   "Not for me, Tamar."
"You think not? Will, now that all's over
And likely we'll not see each other again
Often, nor by ourselves, why shouldn't I tell you . . ."
"What, Tamar?"   "There've been moments . . . hours
    then . . .
When anything you might have asked me for
Would have been given, I'd have done anything
You asked me to, you never asked anything, Will.
I'm telling you this so that you may remember me
As one who had courage to speak truth, you'll meet
So many others."   "But now"—he meant to ask,
"Now it's too late, Tamar?" and hadn't courage,
And Tamar thought "Must I go farther and say more?
Let him despise me as I despise myself.

I have got a little beyond caring." "Now?" she said.
"Do you think I am changed? You have changed, Will, you have grown
Older, and stronger I think, your face is firmer;
And carefuller: I have not changed, I am still reckless
To my own injury, and as trustful as a child.
Would I be with you here in the green thicket
If I weren't trustful? If you should harm me, Will,
I'd think it was no harm." She had laid her hand
On the round sunburnt throat and felt it throbbing,
And while she spoke the thought ran through her mind,
"He is only a little boy but if he turns pale
I have won perhaps, for white's the wanting color.
If he reddens I've lost and it's no matter." He did not move
And seemed not to change color and Tamar said,
"Now I must go. Lee will be home soon.
How soft the ground is in the willow shadow.
I have ended with you honestly, Will; remember me
Not afraid to speak truth and not ashamed
To have stripped my soul naked. You have seen all of me.
Good-by." But when she turned he caught her by the arm,
She sickened inward, thinking, "Now it has come.
I have called and called it and I can't endure it.
Ah. A dumb beast." But he had found words now and said,
"How would you feel, Tamar, if all of a sudden
The bird or star you'd broken your heart to have
Flew into your hands, then flew away. O Tamar, Tamar,
You can't go now, you can't." She unresisting
Took the hot kisses on her neck and hair
And hung loose in his arms the while he carried her
To a clean bank of grass in the deep shadow.
He laid her there and kneeling by her: "You said you trusted me.
You are wise, Tamar; I love you so much too well
I would cut my hands off not to harm you." But she,
Driven by the inward spark of life and dreading
Its premature maturity, could not rest

On harmless love, there were no hands to help
In the innocence of love, and like a vision
Came to her the memory of that other lover
And how he had fallen a farther depth
From firmer innocence at Mal Paso, but the stagnant
Autumn water of Carmel stood too far
From the April freshet in the hills. Tamar pushed off
His kisses and stood up weeping and cried
"It's no use, why will you love me till I cry?
Lee hates you and my father is old and old, we can't
Sour the three years he has before he dies."
"I'll wait for you," said the boy, "wait years, Tamar." Then
    Tamar
Hiding her face against his throat
So that he felt the tears whispered, "But I . . ."
She sobbed, "Have no patience . . . I can't wait. Will . . .
When I made my soul naked for you
There was one spot . . . a fault . . . a shame
I was ashamed to uncover." She pressed her mouth
Between the muscles of his breast: "I want you and want you.
You didn't know that a clean girl could want a man.
Now you will take me and use me and throw me away
And I've . . . earned it." "Tamar, I swear by God .
Never to let you be sorry, but protect you
With all my life." "This is our marriage," Tamar answered.
"But God would have been good to me to have killed me
Before I told you." The boy feeling her body
Vibrant and soft and sweet in its weeping surrender
Went blind and could not feel how she hated him
That moment; when he awakened she was lying
With the auburn hair muddied and the white face
Turned up to the willow leaves, her teeth were bared
And sunk in the under lip, a smear of blood
Reddening the corner of the lips. One of her arms
Crushed both her breasts, the other lay in the grass,
The fingers clutching toward the roots of the soft grass. "O
    Tamar,"

Murmured the boy, "I love you, I love you. What shall I do?
  Go away?
Kill myself, Tamar?" She contracted all her body and
  crouched in the long grass, thinking
"That Helen of my old father's never fooled him at least,"
  and said, "There is nothing to do, nothing.
It is horribly finished. Keep it secret, keep it secret, Will.
  I too was to blame a little.
But I didn't mean . . . this." "I know," he said, "it was
  my fault, I would kill myself, Tamar,
To undo it but I loved you so, Tamar." "Loved? You have
  hurt me and broken me, the house is broken
And any thief can enter it." "O Tamar!" "You have broken
  our crystal innocence, we can never
Look at each other freely again." "What can I do, Tamar?"
  "Nothing. I don't know. Nothing.
Never come to the farm to see me." "Where can I see you,
  Tamar?" "Lee is always watching me,
And I believe he'd kill us. Listen, Will. To-morrow night
  I'll put a lamp in my window,
When all the house is quiet, and if you see it you can climb
  up by the cypress. I must go home,
Lee will be home. Will, though you've done to me worse than
  I ever dreamed, I love you, you have my soul,
I am your tame bird now."

                              VI

This was the high plateau of summer and August waning;
  white vapors
Breathed up no more from the brown fields nor hung in the
  hills; daily the insufferable sun
Rose, naked light, and flaming naked through the pale trans-
  parent ways of the air drained gray
The strengths of nature; all night the eastwind streamed out
  of the valley seaward, and the stars blazed.

The year went up to its annual mountain of death, gilded with
    hateful sunlight, waiting rain.
Stagnant waters decayed, the trickling springs that all the
    misty-hooded summer had fed
Pendulous green under the granite ocean-cliffs dried and
    turned foul, the rock-flowers faded,
And Tamar felt in her blood the filth and fever of the season.
    Walking beside the house-wall
Under her window, she resented sickeningly the wounds in the
    cypress bark, where Andrews
Climbed to his tryst, disgust at herself choked her, and as a
    fire by water
Under the fog-bank of the night lines all the sea and sky with
    fire, so her self-hatred
Reflecting itself abroad burned back against her, all the world
    growing hateful, both her lovers
Hateful, but the intolerably masculine sun hatefullest of all.
    The heat of the season
Multiplied centipedes, the black worms that breed under loose
    rock, they call them thousand-leggers,
They invaded the house, their phalloid bodies cracking under-
    foot with a bad odor, and dropped
Ceiling to pillow at night, a vile plague though not poisonous.
    Also the sweet and female sea
Was weak with calm, one heard too clearly a mounting cormo-
    rant's wing-claps half a mile off shore;
The hard and dry and masculine tyrannized for a season.
    Rain in October or November
Yearly avenges the balance; Tamar's spirit rebelled too soon,
    the female fury abiding
In so beautiful a house of flesh. She came to her aunt the
    ghost-seer. "Listen to me, Aunt Stella.
I think I am going mad, I must talk to the dead; Aunt Stella,
    will you help me?" That old woman
Was happy and proud, no one for years had sought her for
    her talent. "Dear Tamar, I will help you.

We must go down into the darkness, Tamar, it is hard and
painful for me." "I am in the darkness
Already, a fiery darkness." "The good spirits will guide you,
it is easy for you; for me, death.
Death, Tamar, I have to die to reach them." "Death's no
bad thing," she answered, "each hour of the day
Has more teeth." "Are you so unhappy, Tamar, the good
spirits will help you and teach you." "Aunt Stella,
To-night, to-night?" "I groan when I go down to death, your
father and brother will come and spoil it."
"In the evening we will go under the rocks by the sea."
"Well, in the evening." "If they talk to us
I'll buy you black silk and white lace."

      In and out of the little fjord swam the weak waves
Moving their foam in the twilight. Tamar at one flank, old
Stella at the other, upheld poor Jinny
Among the jags of shattered granite, so they came to the
shingle. Rich, damp and dark the sea's breath
Folding them made amend for days of sun-sickness, but Jinny
among the rubble granite
(They had no choice but take her along with them, who else
would care for the idiot?) slipped, and falling
Gashed knees and forehead, and she whimpered quietly in
the darkness. "Here," said Tamar, "I made you
A bed of seaweed under the nose of this old rock, let Jinny
lie beside you, Aunt Stella,
I'll lay the rug over you both." They lay on the odorous kelp,
Tamar squatted beside them,
The weak sea wavered in her rocks and Venus hung over the
west between the cliff-butts
Like the last angel of the world, the crystal night deepening.
The sea and the three women
Kept silence, only Tamar moved herself continually on the
fret of her taut nerves,
And the sea moved, on the obscure bed of her eternity, but
both were voiceless. Tamar

Felt her pulse bolt like a scared horse and stumble and stop,
    for it seemed to her a wandering power
Essayed her body, something hard and rounded and invisible
    pressed itself for entrance
Between the breasts, over the diaphragm. When she was
    forced backward and lay panting, the assault
Failed, the presence withdrew, and in that clearance she
    heard her old Aunt Stella monotonously muttering
Words with no meaning in them; but the tidal night under
    the cliff seemed full of persons
With eyes, although there was no light but the evening planet's
    and her trail in the long water.
Then came a man's voice from the woman, saying, "Que
    quieres pobrecita?" and Tamar, "Morir,"
Trembling, and marveling that she lied for no reason, and
    said, "Es porque no entiendo,
Anything but ingles." To which he answered, "Ah pobrecita,"
    and was silent. And Tamar
Cried, "I will talk to that Helen." But instead another male
    throat spoke out of the woman's
Unintelligible gutturals, and it ceased, and the woman chang-
    ing voice, yet not to her own:
"An Indian. He says his people feasted here and sang to
    their Gods and the tall Gods came walking
Between the tide-marks on the rocks; he says to strip and
    dance and he will sing, and his Gods
Come walking." Tamar answered, crying, "I will not, I will
    not, tell him to go away and let me
Talk to that Helen." But old Stella after a silence: "He says
    No, no, the pregnant women
Would always dance here and the shore belongs to his people's
    ghosts nor will they endure another
Unless they are pleased." And Tamar said, "I cannot dance,
    drive him away," but while she said it
Her hands accepting alien life and a strange will undid the
    fastenings of her garments.

She panted to control them, tears ran down her cheeks, the
    male voice chanted
Hoarse discords from the old woman's body, Tamar drew her
    beauty
Out of its husks; dwellers on eastern shores
Watch moonrises as white as hers
When the half-moon about midnight
Steps out of her husk of water to dance in heaven:
So Tamar weeping
Slipped every sheath down to her feet, the spirt of the place
Ruling her, she and the evening star sharing the darkness,
And danced on the naked shore
Where a pale couch of sand covered the rocks,
Danced with slow steps and streaming hair,
Dark and slender
Against the pallid sea-gleam, slender and maidenly
Dancing and weeping . . .
It seemed to her that all her body
Was touched and troubled with polluting presences
Invisible, and whatever had happened to her from her two
    lovers
She had been until that hour inviolately a virgin,
Whom now the desires of dead men and dead Gods and a
    dead tribe
Used for their common prey . . . dancing and weeping,
Slender and maidenly . . . The chant was changed,
And Tamar's body responded to the change, her spirit
Wailing within her. She heard the brutal voice
And hated it, she heard old Jinny mimic it
In the cracked childish quaver, but all her body
Obeyed it, wakening into wantonness,
Kindling with lust and wilder
Coarseness of insolent gestures,
The senses cold and averse, but the frantic too-governable
    flesh
Inviting the assaults of whatever desired it, of dead men
Or Gods walking the tide-marks,

The beautiful girlish body as gracile as a maiden's
Gone beastlike, crouching and widening,
Agape to be entered, as the earth
Gapes with harsh heat-cracks, the inland adobe of sun-worn
   valleys
At the end of summer
Opening sick mouths for its hope of the rain,
So her body gone mad
Invited the spirits of the night, her belly and her breasts
Twisting, her feet dashed with blood where the granite had
   bruised them,
And she fell, and lay gasping on the sand, on the tide-line.
   Darkness
Possessed the shore when the evening star was down; old
   Stella
Was quiet in her trance; old Jinny the idiot clucked and par-
   roted to herself, there was none but the idiot
Saw whether a God or a troop of Gods came swaggering along
   the tide-marks unto Tamar, to use her
Shamefully and return from her, gross and replete shadows,
   swaggering along the tide-marks
Against the sea-gleam. After a little the life came back to
   that fallen flower; for fear or feebleness
She crept on hands and knees, returning so to the old medium
   of this infamy. Only
The new tide moved in the night now; Tamar with her back
   bent like a bow and the hair fallen forward
Crouched naked at old Stella's feet, and shortly heard the
   voice she had cried for. "I am your Helen.
I would have wished you choose another place to meet me and
   milder ceremonies to summon me.
We dead have traded power for wisdom, yet it is hard for us
   to wait on the maniac living
Patiently, the desires of you wild beasts. You have the
   power." And Tamar murmured, "I had nothing,
Desire nor power." And Helen, "Humbler than you were.
   She has been humbled, my little Tamar.

And not so clean as the first lover left you, Tamar. Another,
and half a dozen savages,
Dead, and dressed up for Gods." "I have endured it," she
answered. Then the sweet disdainful voice
In the throat of the old woman: "As for me, I chose rather
to die." "How can I kill
A dead woman," said Tamar in her heart, not moving the lips,
but the other listened to thought
And answered, "O, we are safe, we shan't fear murder. But,
Tamar, the child will die, and all for nothing
You were submissive by the river, and lived, and endured
fouling. I have heard the wiser flights
Of better spirits, that beat up to the breast and shoulders of
our Father above the star-fire,
Say, 'Sin never buys anything.' " Tamar, kneeling, drew the
thickness of her draggled hair
Over her face and wept till it seemed heavy with blood; and
like a snake lifting its head
Out of a fire, she lifted up her face after a little and said,
"It will live, and my father's
Bitch be proved a liar." And the voice answered, and the
tone of the voice smiled, "Her words
Rhyme with her dancing. Tamar, did you know there were
many of us to watch the dance you danced there,
And the end of the dance? We on the cliff; your mother, who
used to hate me, was among us, Tamar.
But she and I loved each only one man, though it were the
same. We two shared one? You, Tamar,
Are shared by many." And Tamar: "This is your help, I
dug down to you secret dead people
To help me and so I am helped now. What shall I ask more?
How it feels when the last liquid morsel
Slides from the bone? Or whether you see the worm that
burrows up through the eye-socket, or thrill
To the maggot's music in the tube of a dead ear? You stink-
ing dead. That you have no shame

[181]

Is nothing: I have no shame: see I am naked, and if my
    thighs were wet with dead beasts' drippings
I have suffered no pollution like the worms in yours; and if I
    cannot touch you I tell you
There are those I can touch. I have smelled fire and tasted
    fire,
And all these days of horrible sunlight, fire
Hummed in my ears, I have worn fire about me like a cloak
    and burning for clothing. It is God
Who is tired of the house that thousand-leggers crawl about
    in, where an idiot sleeps beside a ghost-seer,
A doting old man sleeps with dead women and does not
    know it,
And pointed bones are at the doors
Or climb up trees to the window. I say He has gathered
Fire all about the walls and no one sees it
But I, the old roof is ripe and the rafters
Rotten for burning, and all the woods are nests of horrible
    things, nothing would ever clean them
But fire, but I will go to a clean home by the good river."
    "You danced, Tamar," replied
The sweet disdainful voice in the mouth of the old woman,
    "and now your song is like your dance,
Modest and sweet. Only you have not said it was you,
Before you came down by the sea to dance,
That lit a candle in your closet and laid
Paper at the foot of the candle. We were watching.
And now the wick is nearly down to the heap,
It's God will have fired the house? But Tamar,
It will not burn. You will have fired it, your brother
Will quench it, I think that God would hardly touch
Anything in that house." "If you know everything,"
Cried Tamar, "tell me where to go.
Now life won't do me and death is shut against me
Because I hate you. O believe me I hate you dead people
More than you dead hate me. Listen to me, Helen.

There is no voice as horrible to me as yours,
And the breasts the worms have worked in. A vicious berry
Grown up out of the graveyard for my poison.
But there is no one in the world as lonely as I,
Betrayed by life and death." Like rain breaking a storm
Sobs broke her voice. Holding by a jag of the cliff
She drew herself full height. God who makes beauty
Disdains no creature, nor despised that wounded
Tired and betrayed body. She in the starlight
And little noises of the rising tide
Naked and not ashamed bore a third part
With the ocean and keen stars in the consistence
And dignity of the world. She was white stone,
Passion and despair and grief had stripped away
Whatever is rounded and approachable
In the body of woman, hers looked hard, long lines
Narrowing down from the shoulder-bones, no appeal,
A weapon and no sheath, fire without fuel,
Saying, "Have you anything more inside you
Old fat and sleepy sepulcher, any more voices?
You can do better than my father's by-play
And the dirty tricks of savages, decenter people
Have died surely. I have so passed nature
That God himself, who's dead or all these devils
Would never have broken hell, might speak out of you
Last season thunder and not scare me." Old Stella
Groaned but not spoke, old Jinny lying beside her
Wakened at the word thunder and suddenly chuckling
Began to mimic a storm, "whoo-whoo" for wind
And "boom-boom-boom" for thunder. Other voices
Wakened far off above the cliff, and suddenly
The farm-bell ringing fire; and on the rock-islets
Sleepy cormorants cried at it. "Why, now He speaks
Another way than out of the fat throat,"
Cried Tamar, and prayed, "O strong and clean and terrible
Spirit and not father punish the hateful house.

Fire eat the walls and roofs, drive the red beast
Through every wormhole of the rotting timbers
And into the woods and into the stable, show them,
These liars, that you are alive." Across her voice
The bell sounded and old Jinny mimicking it,
And shouts above the cliff. "Look, Jinny, look,"
Cried Tamar, "the sky'll be red soon, come and we'll dress
And watch the bonfire." Yet she glanced no thought
At her own mermaid nakedness but gathering
The long black serpents of beached seaweed wove
Wreaths for old Jinny and crowned and wound her.   Mean-
    while
The bell ceased ringing and Stella ceased her moan,
And in the sudden quietness, "Tamar," she said
In the known voice of Helen so many years
Dead, "though you hate me utterly, Tamar, I
Have nothing to give back, I was quite emptied
Of hate and love and the other fires of the flesh
Before your mother gave the clay to my lover
To mould you a vessel to hold them." Tamar, winding
Her mindless puppet in the sea-slough mesh
Said over her shoulder, hardly turning, "Why then
Do you trouble whom you don't hate?" "Because we hunger
And hunger for life," she answered. "Did I come uncalled?
You called me, you have more hot and blind, wild-blooded
And passionate life than any other creature.
How could I ever leave you while the life lasts?
God pity us both, a cataract life
Dashing itself to pieces in an instant.
You are my happiness, you are my happiness and death eats
    you.
I'll leave you when you are empty and cold and join us.
Then pity me, then Tamar, me flitting
The chilly and brittle pumice-tips of the moon,
While the second death
Corrodes this shell of me, till it makes my end."

But Tamar would not listen to her, too busily
Decking old Jinny for the festival fire,
And sighing that thin and envious ghost forsook
Her instrument, and about that time harsh pain
Wrung Tamar's loins and belly, and pain and terror
Expelled her passionate fancies, she cried anxiously,
"Stella, Aunt Stella, help me, will you?" and thinking,
"She hears when Jinny whimpers," twistingly pinched
Her puppet's arm until it screamed. Old Stella
Sat up on the seaweed bed and turned white eyes
No pupils broke the diffused star-gleam in
Upon her sixty-year-old babe, that now
Crouched whimpering, huddled under the slippery leaves
And black whips of the beach; and by it stood gleaming
Tamar, anguished, all white as the blank balls
That swept her with no sight but vision: old Stella
Did not awake yet but a voice blew through her,
Not personal like the other, and shook her body
And shook her hands: "It was no good to do too soon, your
    fire's out, you'd been patient for me
It might have saved two fires." But Tamar: "Stella.
I'm dying: or it is dying: wake up Aunt Stella.
O pain, pain, help me." And the voice: "She is mine while I
    use her. Scream, no one will hear but this one
Who has no mind, who has not more help than July rain."
    And Tamar, "What are you, what are you, mocking me?
More dirt and another dead man? O," she moaned, pressing
    her flanks with both her hands, and bending
So that her hair across her knees lay on the rock. It an-
    swered, "Not a voice from carrion.
Breaker of trees and father of grass, shepherd of clouds and
    waters, if you had waited for me
You'd be the luckier." "What shall I give you," Tamar cried,
    "I have given away——" Pain stopped her, and then
Blood ran, and she fell down on the round stones, and felt nor
    saw nothing. A little later
Old Stella Moreland woke out of her vision, sick and shaking.

[135]

Tamar's mind and suffering
Returned to her neither on the sea-rocks of the midnight nor
    in her own room; but she was lying
Where Lee her brother had lain, nine months before, after his
    fall, in the big westward bedroom.
She lay on the bed, and in one corner was a cot for Stella
    who nursed her, and in the other
A cot for the idiot, whom none else would care for but old
    Stella. After the ache of awakening
And blank dismay of the spirit come home to a spoiled house,
    she lay thinking with vacant wonder
That life is always an old story, repeating itself always like
    the leaves of a tree
Or the lips of an idiot; that herself like Lee her brother
Was picked up bleeding from the sea-bowlders under the sea-
    cliff and carried up to be laid
In the big westward bedroom . . . was he also fouled with
    ghosts before they found him, a gang
Of dead men beating him with rotten bones, mouthing his
    body, piercing him? "Stella," she whispered,
"Have I been sick long?" "There, sweetheart, lie still; three
    or four days." "Has Lee been in to see me?"
"Indeed he has, hours every day." "He'll come, then," and
    she closed her eyes and seemed to sleep.
Someone tapped at the door after an hour and Tamar said,
    "Come, Lee." But her old father
Came in, and he said nothing, but sat down by the bed; Tamar
    had closed her eyes. In a little
Lee entered, and he brought a chair across the room and sat
    by the bed. "Why don't you speak,
Lee?" And he said, "What can I say except I love you,
    sister?" "Why do you call me sister,
Not Tamar?" And he answered, "I love you, Tamar." Then
    old Aunt Stella said, "See, she's much better.
But you must let her rest. She'll be well in a few days; now
    kiss her, Lee, and let her rest."

Lee bent above the white pure cameo-face on the white pillow,
  meaning to kiss the forehead.
But Tamar's hands caught him, her lips reached up for his:
  while Jinny the idiot clapped and chuckled
And made a clucking noise of kisses; then, while Lee sought
  to untwine the arms that yoked his neck,
The old man, rising: "I opened the Book last night thinking
  about the sorrows of this house,
And it said, 'If a man find her in the field and force her and
  lie with her, nevertheless the damsel
Has not earned death, for she cried out and there was none
  to save her.' Be glad, Tamar, my sins
Are only visited on my son, for you there is mercy." "David,
  David,
Will you be gone and let her rest now," cried old Stella, "do
  you mean to kill her with a bible?"
"Woman," he answered, "has God anything to do with you?
  She will not die, the Book
Opened and said it." Tamar, panting, leaned against the
  pillow and said, "Go, go. Tomorrow
Say all you please; what does it matter?" And the old man
  said, "Come, Lee, in the morning she will hear us."
Tamar stretched out her trembling hand, Lee did not touch
  it, but went out ahead of his father.
So they were heard in the hall, and then their foot-steps on
  the stair. Tamar lay quiet and rigid,
With open eyes and tightening fists, with anger like a coiled
  steel spring in her throat but weakness
And pain for the lead weights. After an hour she said, "What
  does he mean to do? Go away?
Kill himself, Stella?" Stella answered, "Nothing, nothing,
  they talk, it's to keep David quiet.
Your father is off his head a little, you know. Now rest you,
  little Tamar, smile and be sleepy,
Scold them to-morrow." "Shut the sun out of my eyes then,"
  Tamar said, but the idiot Jinny

Made such a moaning when the windows were all curtained
  they needed to let in one beam
For dust to dance in; then the idiot and the sick girl slept.
  About the hour of sundown
Tamar was dreaming trivially—an axman chopping down a
  tree and field-mice scampering
Out of the roots—when suddenly like a shift of wind the
  dream
Changed and grew awful, she watched dark horsemen coming
  out of the south, squadrons of hurrying horsemen
Between the hills and the dark sea, helmeted like the soldiers
  of the war in France,
Carrying torches. When they passed Mal Paso Creek the
  columns
Veered, one of the riders said, "Here it began," but another
  answered, "No. Before the granite
Was bedded to build the world on." So they formed and
  galloped north again, hurrying squadrons,
And Tamar thought, "When they come to the Carmel River
  then it will happen. They have passed Mal Paso."

                                          Meanwhile—
Who has ever guessed to what odd ports, what sea buoying
  the keels, a passion blows its bulkless
Navies of vision? High up in the hills
Ramon Ramirez, who was herdsman of the Cauldwell herds,
  stood in his cabin doorway
Rolling a cigarette a half-hour after sundown, and he felt
  puffs from the south
Come down the slope of stunted redwoods, so he thought the
  year was turning at last, and shortly
There would come showers; he walked therefore a hundred
  yards to westward, where a point of the hill
Stood over Wildcat Canyon and the sea was visible; he saw
  Point Lobos gemmed in the darkening
Pale yellow sea; and on the point the barn-roofs and the
  house-roof breaking up through the blackness

Of twilight cypress tops, and over the sea a cloud forming.
    The evening darkened. Southwestward
A half-mile loop of the coast-road could be seen, this side
    Mal Paso. Suddenly a nebular company
Of lights rounded the hill, Ramirez thought the headlights
    of a car sweeping the road,
But in a moment saw that it was horsemen, each carrying a
    light, hurrying northward,
Moving in squads he judged of twenty or twenty-five, he
    counted twelve or thirteen companies
When the brush broke behind him and a horseman rode the
    headlong ridge like level ground,
Helmeted, carrying a torch. Followed a squad of twelve,
    helmeted, cantering the headlong ridge
Like level ground. He thought in the nervous innocence
    of the early war, they must be Germans.

Tamar awoke out of her dream and heard old Jinny saying,
    "Dear sister Helen, kiss me
As you kiss David. I was watching under a rock, he took your
    clothes off and you kissed him
So hard and hard, I love you too, Helen; you hardly ever
    kiss me." Tamar lay rigid,
Breathless to listen to her; it was well known in the house
    that under the shell of imbecility
Speech and a spirit however subdued existed still; there
    were waking flashes, and more often
She talked in sleep and proved her dreams were made out of
    clear memories, childhood sights and girlhood
Fancies, before the shadow had fallen; so Tamar craving food
    for passion listened to her,
And heard: "Why are you cross, Helen? I won't peek if
    you'd rather I didn't. Darling Helen,
I love him, too; I'd let him play with me the way he does
    with you if he wanted to.
And Lily and Stella hate me as much as they hate you." All
    she said after was so mumbled

[139]

That Tamar could not hear it, could only hear the mumble,
    and old Aunt Stella's nasal sleep
And the sea murmuring. When the mumbled voice was quiet
    it seemed to Tamar
A strange thing was preparing, an inward pressure
Grew in her throat and seemed to swell her arms and hands
And join itself with a fluid power
Streaming from somewhere in the room—from Jinny?
From Stella?—and in a moment the heavy chair
That Lee had sat in, tipped up, rose from the floor,
And floated to the place he had brought it from
Five hours ago. The power was then relaxed,
And Tamar could breathe and speak. She awaked old Stella
And trembling told her what she had seen; who laughed
And answered vaguely so that Tamar wondered
Whether she was still asleep, and let her burrow
In her bed again and sleep. Later that night
Tamar too slept, but shudderingly, in snatches,
For fear of dreaming. A night like years. In the gray of
    morning
A horse screamed from the stableyard and Tamar
Heard the thud of hoofs lashing out and timbers
Splintering, and two or three horses broken loose
Galloped about the grounds of the house. She heard men
    calling,
And down-stairs Lee in a loud angry tone
Saying "Someone's pitched the saw-buck and the woodpile
Into the horse-corral." Then Tamar thought
"The same power moved his chair in the room, my hatred,
    my hatred,
Disturbing the house because I failed to burn it.
I must be quiet and quiet and quiet and keep
The serving spirits of my hid hatred quiet
Until my time serves too. Helen you shadow
Were never served so handily." Stella had awakened,
And Tamar asking for a drink of water
She waddled to fetch it and met Lee at the door.

"O Lee," she said, "that noise—what ever has happened?"
He: "I don't know. Some fool has pitched the whole woodpile
Into the horse-corral. Is Tamar awake?
I want to see Tamar." He entered the room
As Stella left it. Old withered Aunt Jinny
Sat up in her bed saying "David, David," but Lee
Kneeling at Tamar's bedside, "O Tamar, Tamar.
The old man's out-doors tottering after the horses
So I can see you a minute. O why, why, why,
Didn't you tell me Tamar? I'd have taken you up
In my arms and carried you to the end of the world."
"How it's turned sour," she thought, "I'd have been glad of this
Yesterday," and she clinched her finger-nails
Into her palms under the bed-covers,
Saying, "Tell you—what? What have they told you," she asked
With a white sidelong smile, "people are always lying?"
"Tamar, that you—that we . . . O I've lived hell
Four or five days now." "You look well enough,"
She answered, "put yours by mine," laying her white, lean,
And somewhat twitching hand on the counterpane,
"Mine used to manage a bridle as well as yours
And now look at them. I don't suppose you want me
Now, but it doesn't matter. You used to come to my bed
With something else than pity, convenient, wasn't it?
Not having to ride to Monterey?" He answered frowning,
"However much you hurt me I am very glad too
That all the joys and memories of a love
As great and as forbidden as ours are nothing to you
Or worse than nothing, because I have to go away,
Two days from now, and stay till the war's over
And you are married and father is dead. I've promised him
Never to see him again, never to see his face.
He didn't ask it because he thinks his Book
Told him I'm to be killed. That's foolishness,

[141]

But makes your peace with him and thank God for that.
What his Book told him." "So here's the secret
I wasn't strong enough yesterday to hear.
I thought maybe you meant to kill yourself."
"Thanks, Tamar. The old man thinks I don't need to." "O,
You beast," she said, "you runaway dog.
I wish you joy of your dirty Frenchwomen
You want instead of me. Take it, take it.
Old people in their dotage gabble the truth,
You won't live long." "What can I say, Tamar?
I'm sorry, I'm sorry, I'm sorry." "But go away,"
She said, "and if you'll come again to-night
Maybe I'll tell you mine, my secret."
               That morning
Ramon Ramirez who watched the Cauldwell cattle
Up in the hills kept thinking of his vision
Of helmets carrying torches; he looked for tracks
On the ridge where he had seen the riders cantering,
And not a bush was broken, not a hoof-mark
Scarred the sear grass. At noon he thought he'd ride
To Vogel's place taking his lunch in the saddle
And tell someone about it. At the gap in the hill
Where storm-killed redwoods line both sides he met
Johnny Cabrera with a flaming bundle
Of dead twigs and dry grass tied with brown cord.
He smelled the smoke and saw the flame sag over
On a little wind from the east, and said in Spanish
"Eh Johnny, are you out of matches?" who answered flashing
His white teeth in a smile, "I'm carrying fire to Lobos
If God is willing," and walked swinging ahead,
Singing to himself the fool south-border couplet
"No tengo tabaco, no tengo papel,
No tengo dinero, God damn it to hell,"
And Ramon called "Hey Johnny," but he would not stop
Nor answer, and thinking life goes wild at times
Ramon came to the hill-slope under Vogel's
And smelled new smoke and saw the clouds go up

And this same Johnny with two other men
Firing the brush to make spring pasture. Ramon
Felt the scalp tighten on his temples and thought best
Not to speak word of either one of his visions,
Though he talked with the men, they told him Tamar
    Cauldwell
Was sick, and Lee had enlisted.
                    The afternoon
Was feverish for so temperate a sea-coast
And terribly full of light, the sea like a hard mirror
Reverberated the straight and shining serpents
That fell from heaven and Tamar dreamed in a doze
She was hung naked by that tight cloth bandage
Half-way between sea and sky, beaten on by both,
Burning with light; wakening she found she had tumbled
The bed-clothes to the floor and torn her night-gown
To rags, and was alone in the room, and blinded
By the great glare of sun in the western windows.
She rose and shut the curtains though they had told her
She mustn't get out of bed, and finding herself
Able to walk she stood by the little window
That looked southeast from the south bay of the room
And saw the smoke of burning brushwood slopes
Tower up out of the hills in the windless weather
Like an enormous pinetree, "Everybody
But me has luck with fire," she thought to herself,
"But I can walk now," and returned to bed
And drew the sheets over her flanks, but leaving
The breasts and the shoulders bare. In half an hour
Stella and old Jinny came into the room
With the old man David Cauldwell. Stella hastily
Drew up the sheet to Tamar's throat but Tamar
Saying, "You left the curtains open and the sun
Has nearly killed me," doubled it down again,
And David Cauldwell, trembling: "Will you attempt
Age and the very grave, uncovering your body

To move the old bones that seventy years have broken
And dance your bosoms at me through a mist of death?
Though I know that you and your brother have utterly de-
spised
The bonds of blood, and daughter and father are no closer
bound,
And though this house spits out all goodness, I am old, I am
old, I am old,
What do you want of me?" He stood tottering and wept,
Covering his eyes and beard with shaken old hands,
And Tamar, having not moved, "Nothing," she said,
"Nothing, old man. I have swum too deep into the mud
For this to sicken me; and as you say, there are neither
Brother nor sister, daughter nor father, nor any love
This side the doorways of the damnable house.
But I have a wildbeast of a secret hidden
Under the uncovered breast will eat us all up
Before Lee goes." "It is a lie, it is a lie, it is all a lie.
Stella you must go out, go out of the room Stella,
Not to hear the sick and horrible imaginations
A sick girl makes for herself. Go Stella." "Indeed I won't,
David." "You—you—it is still my house." "To let you kill
her with bad words
All out of the bible—indeed I won't." "Go, Stella," said
Tamar,
"Let me talk to this old man, and see who has suffered
When you come back. I am out of pity, and you and Jinny
Will be less scorched on the other side of the door." After
a third refusal
The old woman went, leading her charge, and Tamar: "You
thought it was your house? It is me they obey.
It is mine, I shall destroy it. Poor old man I have earned
authority." "You have gone mad," he answered.
And she: "I'll show you our trouble, you sinned, your old
book calls it, and repented: that was foolish.
I was unluckier, I had no chance to repent, so I learned
something, we must keep sin pure

Or it will poison us, the grain of goodness in a sin is poison.
Old man, you have no conception

Of the freedom of purity. Lock the door, old man, I am
telling you a secret." But he trembling,

"O God thou hast judged her guiltless, the Book of thy word
spake it, thou hast the life of the young man

My son . . ." and Tamar said, "Tell God we have revoked
relationship in the house, he is not

Your son nor you my father." "Dear God, blot out her words,
she has gone mad. Tamar, I will lock it,

Lest anyone should come and hear you, and I will wrestle
for you with God, I will not go out

Until you are His." He went and turned the key and Tamar
said, "I told you I have authority.

You obey me like the others, we pure have power. Perhaps
there are other ways, but I was plunged

In the dirt of the world to win it, and, O father, so I will
call you this last time, dear father

You cannot think what freedom and what pleasure live in
having abjured laws, in having

Annulled hope, I am now at peace." "There is no peace,
there is none, there is none, there is no peace

But His," he stammered, "but God's." "Not in my arms, old
man, on these two little pillows? Your son

Found it there, and another, and dead men have defiled me
You that are half dead and half living,

Look, poor old man. That Helen of yours, when you were
young, where was her body more desirable,

Or was she lovinger than I? You know it is forty years
ago that we revoked

Relationships in the house." "He never forgives, He never
forgives, evil punishes evil

With the horrible mockery of an echo." "Is the echo louder
than the voice, I have surpassed her,

Yours was the echo, time stands still old man, you'll learn
when you have lived at the muddy root

Under the rock of things; all times are now, to-day plays on
last year and the inch of our future
Made the first morning of the world. You named me for
the monument in a desolate graveyard,
Fool, and I say you were deceived, it was out of me that
fire lit you and your Helen, your body
Joined with your sister's
Only because I was to be named Tamar and to love my
brother and my father.
I am the fountain." But he, shuddering, moaned, "You have
gone mad, you have gone mad, Tamar,"
And twisted his old hands muttering, "I fear hell. O Tamar,
the nights I have spent in agony,
Ages of pain, when the eastwind ran like glass under the
peeping stars or the southwest wind
Plowed in the blackness of the tree. You—a little thing has
driven you mad, a moment of suffering,
But I for more than forty years have lain under the mountains
and looked down into hell."
"One word," she said, "that was not written in the book of
my fears. I did indeed fear pain
Before peace found me, or death, never that dream. Old
man, to be afraid is the only hell
And dead people are quit of it, I have talked with the dead."
"Have you—with her?" "Your pitiful Helen?
She is always all about me; if you lay in my arms old man
you would be with her. Look at me,
Have you forgotten—your Helen?" He in torture
Groaned like a beast, but when he approached the bed she
laughed, "Not here, behind you." And he blindly
Clutching at her, she left the coverlet in his hands and slip-
ping free at the other side
Saw in a mirror on the wall her own bright throat and
shoulder and just beyond them the haggard
Open-mouthed mask, the irreverend beard and blind red eyes.
She caught the mirror from its fastening

And held it to him, reverse. "Here is her picture, Helen's
   picture, look at her, why is she always
Crying and crying?" When he turned the frame and looked,
   then Tamar: "See that is her lover's.
The hairy and horrible lips to kiss her, the drizzling eyes to
   eat her beauty, happiest of women
If only he were faithful; he is too young and wild and lovely,
   and the lusts of his youth
Lead him to paw strange beds." The old man turned the
   glass and gazed at the blank side, and turned it
Again face towards him, he seemed drinking all the vision in
   it, and Tamar: "Helen, Helen,
I know you are here present; was I humbled in the night
   lately and you exulted?
See here your lover. I think my mother will not envy you
   now, your lover, Helen, your lover,
The mouth to kiss you, the hands to fondle secret places."
   Then the old man sobbing, "It is not easy
To be old, mocked, and a fool." And Tamar, "What, not
   yet, you have not gone mad yet? Look, old fellow.
These rags drop off, the bandages hid something but I'm done
   with them. See . . . I am the fire
Burning the house." "What do you want, what do you
   want?" he said, and stumbled toward her, weeping.
"Only to strangle a ghost and to destroy the house. Spit on
   the memory of that Helen
You might have anything of me." And he groaning, "When
   I was young
I thought it was my fault, I am old and know it was hers,
   night after night, night after night
I have lain in the dark, Tamar, and cursed her." "And now?"
   "I hate her, Tamar." "O," said Tamar gently,
"It is enough, she has heard you. Now unlock the door, old
   father, and go, and go." "Your promise,
Tamar, the promise, Tamar." "Why I might do it, I have no
   feeling of revolt against it.

[147]

Though you have forgotten that fear of hell why should I let
   you
Be mocked by God?" And he, the stumpage of his teeth
   knocking together, "You think, you think
I'll go to the stables and a rope from a rafter
Finish it for you?" "Dear, I am still sick," she answered,
   "you don't want to kill me? A man
Can wait three days: men have lived years and years on
   the mere hope."
                        Meanwhile the two old women
Sat in their room, old Stella sat at the window looking south
   into the cypress boughs, and Jinny
On her bed's edge, rocking her little withered body backward
   and forward, and said vacantly,
"Helen, what do you do the times you lock the door to be
   alone, and Lily and Stella
Wonder where David's ridden to?" After a while she said
   again, "Do tell me, sister Helen,
What you are doing the times you lock the door to be alone,
   and Lily and Stella wonder
Where David's ridden to?" And a third time she repeated,
   "Darling sister Helen, tell me
What you are doing the times you lock the door to be alone,
   and Lily and Stella wonder
Where David's riding?" Stella seemed to awake, catching
   at breath, and not in her own voice,
"What does she mean," she said, "my picture, picture? O!
   the mirror—I read in a book Jinny.
A story about lovers; I never had a lover, I read about them;—
   I won't look, though.
With all that blind abundance, so much of life and blood,
   that sweet and warming blaze of passion,
She has also a monkey in her mind." "Tell me the story
   about the picture." "Ugh, if she plans
To humble herself utterly . . . You may peek, Jinny,
Try if you can, shut both eyes, draw them back into your
   forehead, and look, look, look

[148]

Over the eyebrows, no, like this, higher up, up where the
  hairs grows, now peek Jinny. Can't you
See through the walls? You can. Look, look, Jinny. As if
  they'd cut a window. I used to tell you
That God could see into caves: you are like God now: peek,
  Jinny." "I can see something.
It's in the stable, David's come from Monterey, he's hanging
  the saddle on a peg there . . ."
"Jinny, I shall be angry. That's not David,
It's Lee, don't look into the stable, look into the bedroom,
  you know, Jinny, the bedroom,
Where we left Tamar on the bed." "O that's too near, it
  hurts me, it hurts my head, don't scold me, Helen.
How can I see if I'm crying? I see now clearly."
"What do you see?" "I see through walls, O, I'm like God,
  Helen. I see the wood and plaster
And see right through them." "What? What are they
  doing?" "How can you be there and here, too, Helen?"
"It's Tamar, what is she doing?" "I know it's you Helen,
  because you have no hair
Under the arms, I see the blue veins under the arms." "Well,
  if it's me, what is she doing?
Is she on the bed? What is she saying?" "She is on fire
  Helen, she has white fire all around you
Instead of clothes, and that is why you are laughing with so
  pale a face." "Does she let him do
Whatever he wants to, Jinny?" "He says that he hates . . .
  somebody . . . and then you laughed for he had a rope
Around his throat a moment, the beard stuck out over it."
  "O Jinny it wasn't I that laughed,
It was that Tamar, Tamar, Tamar, she has bought him for
  nothing. She and her mother both to have him,
The old hollow fool." "What do they want him for, Helen?"
  "To plug a chink, to plug a chink, Jinny,
In the horrible vanity of women. Lee's come home, now I
  could punish her, she's past hurting,

Are they huddled together Jinny?   What, not yet, not yet?"
    "You asked for the key but when he held it
You ran away from him."   "What do I want, what do I
    want, it is frightful to be dead, what do I . . .
Without power, and no body or face.   To kill her, kill her?
There's no hell and curse God for it . . ."

                    Lee Cauldwell childishly
Loved hearing the spurs jingle, and because he felt
"After to-morrow I shan't wear them again,
Nor straddle a pony for many a weary month and year,
Maybe forever," he left them at his heels
When he drew off the chaps and hung the saddle
On the oak peg in the stable-wall.   He entered the house
Slowly, he had taken five drinks in Monterey
And saw his tragedy of love, sin, and war
At the disinterested romantic angle
Misted with not unpleasing melancholy,
Over with, new adventure ahead, a perilous cruise
On the other ocean, and great play of guns
On the other shore . . . at the turn of the stair he heard
Hands hammering a locked door, and a voice unknown to
    him
Crying, "Tamar, I loved you for your flame of passion
And hated you for its deeds, all that we dead
Can love or hate with: and now will you crust flame
With filth, submit?   Submit?   Tamar,
The defilement of the tideline dead was nothing
To this defilement."   Then Lee jingling his spurs,
Jumped four steps to the landing, "Who is there?   You,
Aunt Stella?"   Old gray Aunt Jinny like a little child
Moaning drew back from him, and the mouth of Stella:
"A man that's ready to cross land and water
To set the world in order can't be expected
To leave his house in order."   And Lee, "Listen, Aunt Stella,
Who are you playing, I mean what voice out of the world of
    the dead

Is speaking from you?" She answered, "Nothing.   I was something
Forty years back but now I'm only the bloodhound
To bay at the smell of what they're doing in there."
"Who? Tamar? Blood?"   "Too close in blood, I am the blood-stain
On the doorsill of a crime, she does her business
Under her own roof mostly."   "Tamar, Tamar,"
Lee called, shaking the door. She from within
Answered "I am here, Lee. Have you said good-by
To Nita and Conchita in Monterey
And your fat Fanny? But who is the woman at the door
Making the noise?"   He said, "Open the door;
Open the door, Tamar."   And she, "I opened it for you,
You are going to France to knock at other doors.
I opened it for you and others."   "What others?"   "Ask her,"
Said the young fierce voice from old Aunt Stella's lips,
"What other now?"   "She is alone there," he answered,
"A devil is in you. Tamar," he said, "tell her
You are alone."   "No, Lee, I am asking in earnest,
Who is the woman making the noise out there?
Someone you've brought from Monterey? Tell her to go:
Father is here."   "Why have you locked it, why have you locked it?"
He felt the door-knob turning in his hand
And the key shook the lock; Tamar stood in the doorway
Wrapped in a loose blue robe that the auburn hair
Burned on, and beyond her the old man knelt by the bed,
His face in the lean twisted hands. "He was praying for me,"
Tamar said quietly. "You are leaving to-morrow,
He has only one child."   Then the old man lifting a face
From which the flesh seemed to have fallen, and the eyes
Dropped and been lost: "What will you do to him, Tamar?
Tamar, have mercy.
He was my son, years back."   She answered, "I am glad
That you know who has power in the house"; and he
Hid the disfigured face, between his wrists,

The beard kept moving, they thought him praying to God.
And Tamar said, "It is coming to the end of the bad story,
That needn't have been bad only we fools
Botch everything, but a dead fool's the worst,
This old man's sister who rackets at the doors
And drove me mad, although she is nothing but a voice,
Dead, shelled, and the shell rotted, but she had to meddle
In the decencies of life here. Lee, if you truly
Lust for the taste of a French woman I'll let you go
For fear you die unsatisfied and plague
Somebody's children with a ghost's hungers
Forty years after death. Do I care, do I care?
You shan't go, Lee. I told the old man I have a secret
That will eat us all up . . . and then, dead woman,
What will you have to feed on? You spirits flicker out
Too speedily, forty years is a long life for a ghost
And you will only famish a little longer
To whom I'd wish eternity." "O Tamar, Tamar,"
It answered out of Stella's mouth, "has the uttermost
Not taught you anything yet, not even that extinction
Is the only terror?" "You lie too much," she answered,
"You'll enter it soon and not feel any stitch
Of fear afterwards. Listen, Lee, your arms
Were not the first man's to encircle me, and that spilled life
Losing which let me free to laugh at God,
I think you had no share in." He trembled, and said
"O Tamar has your sickness and my crime
Cut you so deep? A lunatic in a dream
Dreams nearer things than this." "I'd never have told you,"
She answered, "if his vicious anger—after I'd balanced
Between you a long time and then chose you—
Hadn't followed his love's old'night-way to my window
And kindled fire in, the room when I was gone,
The spite-fire that might easily have eaten up
And horribly, our helpless father, or this innocent
Jinny . . ." "He did it, he did it, forgive me, Tamar.
I thought that you gone mad . . . Tamar, I know

[152]

That you believe what you are saying but I
Do not believe you. There was no one." "The signal
Was a lamp in the window, perhaps some night
He'd come still if you'd set a lamp into my window.
And when he climbed out of the cypress tree
Then you would know him." "I would mark him to know.
But it's not true." "Since I don't sleep there now
You might try for the moth; if he doesn't come
I'll tell you·his name to-morrow." Then the old man jerking
Like dry bones wired pulled himself half erect
With clutching at the bed-clothes: "Have mercy, Tamar.
Lee, there's a trick in it, she is a burning fire,
She is packed with death. I have learned her, I have learned
    her, I have learned her,
Too cruel to measure strychnine, too cunning-cruel
To snap a gun, aiming ourselves against us."
Lee answered, "There is almost nothing here to understand.
If we all did wrong why have we all gone mad
But me, I haven't a touch of it. Listen, dead woman,
Do you feel any light here?" "Fire—as much light
As a bird needs," the voice from the old woman
Answered, "I am the gull on the butt of the mast
Watching the ship founder, I'll fly away home
When you go down, or a swallow above a chimney
Watching the brick and mortar fly in the earthquake."
"I'll just go look at the young cypress bark
Under her window," he said, "it might have taken
The bite of a thief's hob-nails." When he was gone
And jingling down the stair, then Tamar: "Poor people,
Why do you cry out so? I have three witnesses,
The old man that died to-day, and a dead woman
Forty years dead, and an idiot, and only one of you
Decently quiet. There is the great and quiet water
Reaching to Asia, and in an hour or so
The still stars will show over it but I·am quieter
Inside than even the ocean or the stars.
Though I have to kindle paper flares of passion

Sometimes, to fool you with. But I was thinking
Last night, that people all over the world
Are doing much worse and suffering much more than we
This wartime, and the stars don't wink, and the ocean
Storms perhaps less than usual." Then the dead woman,
"Wild life, she has touched the ice-core of things and learned
Something, that frost burns worse than fire." "O, it's not
   true,"
She answered, "frost is kind; why, almost nothing
You say is true. Helen, do you remember at all
The beauty and strangeness of this place? Old cypresses
The sailor wind works into deep-sea knots
A thousand years; age-reddened granite
That was the world's cradle and crumbles apieces
Now that we're all grown up, breaks out at the roots;
And underneath it the old gray-granite strength
Is neither glad nor sorry to take the seas
Of all the storms forever and stand as firmly
As when the red hawk wings of the first dawn
Streamed up the sky over it: there is one more beautiful thing,
Water that owns the north and west and south
And is all colors and never is all quiet,
And the fogs are its breath and float along the branches of
   the cypresses.
And I forgot the coals of ruby lichen
That glow in the fog on the old twigs. To live here
Seventy-five years or eighty, and have children,
And watch these things fill up their eyes, would not
Be a bad life . . . I'd rather be what I am,
Feeling this peace and joy, the fire's joy's burning,
And I have my peace." Then the old man in the dull
And heartless voice answered, "The strangest thing
Is that He never speaks: we know we are damned, why should
   He speak? The book
Is written already. Cauldwell, Cauldwell, Cauldwell, Cauld-
   well.

Eternal death, eternal wrath, eternal torture, eternity, eter-
nity, eternity . . .
That's after the judgment." "You needn't have any fear,
old father,
Of anything to happen after to-morrow," Tamar answered,
"we have turned every page
But the last page, and now our paper's so worn out and tissuey
I can read it already
Right through the leaf, print backwards."

It was twilight in the room, the shiny side of the wheel
Dipping toward Asia; and the year dipping toward winter
encrimsoned the grave spokes of sundown;
And jingling in the door Lee Cauldwell with the day's-death
flush upon his face: "Father:
There are marks on the cypress: a hell of a way to send your
soldier off: I want to talk to her
Alone. You and the women——" he flung his hand out,
meaning "go." The old man without speaking
Moved to the door, propping his weakness on a chair and on
the door-frame, and Lee entering
Passed him and the two women followed him—three, if Stella
were one—but when they had passed the doorway
Old Cauldwell turned, and tottering in it: "Death is the
horror," he said, "nothing else lasts, pain passes,
Death's the only trap. I am much too wise to swing myself
in the stable on a rope from a rafter. Helen, Helen,
You know about death." "It is cold," she answered from
the hallway; "unspeakably hopeless . . ."
"You curse of talkers,
Go," he said, and he shut the door against them and said,
"Slut, how many, how many?" She, laughing,
"I knew you would be sweet to me: I am still sick: did you
find marks in the bark? I am still sick, Lee;
You don't intend killing me?" "Flogging, whipping, whip-
ping, is there anything male about here

You haven't used yet? Agh you mouth, you open mouth. But
  I won't touch you." "Let me say something,"
She answered, standing dark against the west in the window,
  the death of the winter rose of evening
Behind her little high-poised head, and threading the brown
  twilight of the room with the silver
Exultance of her voice, "My brother can you feel how happy
  I am but how far off too?
If I have done wrong it has turned good to me, I could almost
  be sorry that I have to die now
Out of such freedom; if I were standing back of the evening
  crimson on a mountain in Asia
All the fool shames you can whip up into a filth of words would
  not be farther off me,
Nor any fear of anything, if I stood in the evening star and
  saw this dusty dime's worth
A dot of light, dropped up the star-gleam. Poor brother, poor
  brother, you played the fool too
But not enough, it is not enough to taste delight and passion
  and disgust and loathing
And agony, you have to be wide alive, 'an open mouth' you
  said, all the while, to reach this heaven
You'll never grow up to. Though it's possible if I'd let you
  go asoldiering, there on the dunghills
Of death and fire . . . ah, you'd taste nothing even there
  but the officers' orders, beef and brandy,
And the tired bodies of a few black-eyed French dance-girls:
  it is better for you
To be lost here than there." "You are up in the evening
  star," he said, "you can't feel this," flat-handed
Striking her cheek, "you are up on a mountain in Asia, who
  made you believe that you could keep me
Or let me go? I am going to-morrow, to-night I set the
  house in order." "There is nothing now
You can be sorry for," she answered, "not even this, it is out
  of the count, the cup ran over

Yesterday." He turned and left the room, the foolish tune
  of the spurs tinkled
Hallway and stair. Tamar, handling the fiery spot upon her
  cheek smiled in the darkness.
Feeling so sure of the end. "Night after night he has ridden
  to the granite at the rivermouth
And missed my light, to-night he will see it, the Lobos star
  he called it, and look and look to be sure
It is not a ship's light nor a star's, there in the south, then
  he will come, and my three lovers
Under one roof."

VII

Lee Cauldwell felt his way in the dark among the cypress
  trees, and turning
At the stable-door saw the evening star, he felt for the lantern
Hung on the bent nail to the right of the door,
Lighted it, and in the sweet hay-dusty darkness
Found the black quirt that hung beside the saddle
And seemed a living snake in the hand, then he opened
A locker full of hunter's gear and tumbled
Leather and iron to the floor for an old sheath-knife
Under all the rest; he took the knife and whip
And Tamar in the dark of the westward bedroom heard him
Tinkle on the stair and jingle in the hall, slow steps
Moving to hers, the room that had been her room
Before this illness; she felt him as if she had been there
Lighting her lamp and setting it on the sill,
Then felt him look about the little room and feel it
Breathing and warm with her once habitancy
And the hours of hers and his there, and soften almost
To childish tears at trifles on the wall;
And then he would look at the bed and stiffen
In a brittle rage, feel with thrust under-lip
Virtuous, an outcrop of morality in him
To grow ridiculous and wish to be cruel,

And so return to her. Hastily, without light,
She redded up some of the room's untidiness,
Thrust into the stove the folds of bandage-cloth,
Straightened the bed a little, and laying aside
The loose blue robe lay down in the bed to await him,
Who, throwing open the door, "Tamar: I've got no right
To put my hands into your life, I see
That each of us lives only a little while
And must do what he can with it: so, I'm going
To-night; I'd nearly worked myself to the act
Of some new foolishness: are you there, Tamar?
The lamp?" He struck a match and saw her eyes
Shine on him from the pillow and when the lamp
Was lighted he began again: "It's all such foolishness.
Well, you and I are done. I set your lamp for a signal on
    the sill,
I'll take it away or help you to that room,
Whichever you like. That'll be my last hand in the game.
It won't take me ten minutes to pack and go, my plan's
Not to risk losing temper and have half-decent
Thoughts of you while I'm gone, and you of me, Tamar."
She lay too quietly and the shining eyes
Seemed not to hide amusement, he waited for her
To acknowledge not in direct words perhaps
His generosity, but she silent, "Well, shall I leave the lamp?"
He said, not all so kindly, and Tamar, "I've no one else
If you are going. But if you'd stay I wouldn't
Touch you again, ever. Agh, you can't wait
To get to France to crawl into strange beds,
But Monterey to-night. You—what a beast.
You like them dirty." He said, "You're a fool, Tamar.
Well, so I'll leave the lamp. Good-by, Tamar."
"You said you'd help me down the hall." "Yes, even that.
What must I do, carry you?" "Is the bed together?
See whether there are sheets and covers on it."
He went, and returned icy-pale. "It hasn't been changed
Since I smelled fire and ran into the room

[158]

Six or eight days ago. The cupboard door-frame
Is all charcoal. By God, Tamar,
If I believed he'd done it—who is he, Andrews?—
You and your lies have made a horror in the house.
What, shall I go, shall I go?" "Me? who made *me*
Believe that I could keep you or let you go,
Didn't you say?" "You still believe it," he answered,
Doubling his fists to hold in anger, the passionate need
Of striking her like a torrent in his throat,
"Believe it, fool." "Poor brother. You will never see France,
Never wear uniform nor learn how to fasten
A bayonet to a gun-barrel." "Come. Stop talking.
Get up, come to your room." "Carry me," she answered.
"Though I am not really much too tired to walk.
You used to like me." "Well, to get done and be gone,"
He said, bending above her, she enlaced his neck
Softly and strongly and raised her knees to let
His arm slip under them, he like a man stung by a serpent
Felt weakness and then rage, panted to lift her
And staggered in the doorway and in the dark hallway
Grew dizzy, and difficultly went on and groaning
Dropped her on the bed in her own room, she did not move
To cover herself, then he drawing his palm
Across his forehead found it streaming wet
And said, "You whore, you whore, you whore. Well, you
    shall have it,
You've earned it," and he twisted himself to the little table
And took the whip, the oiled black supple quirt,
Loaded at the handle, that seemed a living snake in the hand,
And felt the exasperate force of his whole baffled
And blindfold life flow sideways into the shoulder
Swinging it, and half repenting while it dropped
Sickened to see the beautiful bare white
Blemishless body writhe under it before it fell,
The loins pressed into the bed, the breast and head
Twisting erect, and at the noise of the stroke
He made a hoarse cry in his throat but she

Took it silently, and lay still afterward,
Her head so stricken backward that the neck
Seemed strained to breaking, the coppery pad of her hair
Crushed on the shoulder-blades, while that red snake-trail
Swelled visibly from the waist and flank down the left thigh.
"O God, God, God," he groaned; and she, her whole body
Twitching on the white bed whispered between her teeth
"It was in the bargain," and from her bitten lip
A trickle of blood ran down to the pillow.

                    That one light in the room,
The lamp on the sill, did not turn redder for blood nor with
     the whipstripe
But shone serene and innocent up the northward night, writ-
     ing a long pale-golden track
In the river's arm of sea, and beyond the river's mouth where
     the old lion's teeth of blunted granite
Crop out of the headland young Will Andrews kissed it with
     his eyes, rode south and crossed the river's
Late-summer sand-lock. Figures of fire moved in the hills
     on the left, the pasture-fires and brush-fires
Men kindle before rain, on a southerly wind the smell of the
     smoke reached him, the sea on his right
Breathed; when he skirted the darkness of the gum-tree grove
     at San Jose creek-mouth he remembered
Verdugo killed there; Sylvia Vierra and her man had lived in
     the little white-washed farm-hut
Under the surf-reverberant blue-gums; two years ago they
     had had much wine in the house, their friend
Verdugo came avisiting, he being drunk on the raw plenty of
     wine they thought abused
Nine-year-old Mary, Sylvia's daughter, they struck him from
     behind and when he was down unmanned him
With the kitchen knife, then plotted drunkenly—for he seemed
     to be dead—where to dispose the body.
That evening Tamar Cauldwell riding her white pony along
     the coast-road saw a great bonfire

Periling the gum-tree grove, and riding under the smoke met
    evil odors, turning in there
Saw by the firelight a man's feet hang out of the fire; then
    Tamar never having suffered
Fear in her life, knocked at the hut's door and unanswered
    entered, and found the Vierras asleep
Steaming away their wine, but little Mary weeping. She had
    taken the child and ridden homeward.
Young Andrews thinking of that idyll of the country gulped
    at the smoke from the hills and tethered
His horse in the hiding of a clump of pines, and climbed the
    line-fence.
               Turning a cypress thicket
He saw a figure sway in the starlight, and stood still, breath-
    less. A woman: Tamar? Not Tamar:
No one he knew: it faced the east gables of the house and
    seemed twisting its hands and suddenly
Flung up both arms to its face and passed out of the patch
    of starlight. The boy, troubled and cautious,
Turned the other way and circling to the south face of the
    house peered from behind the buttressed
Base of a seventy-year-old trunk that yellow light on the
    other side clothed, and he saw
A lamp on the table and three people sitting by it; the old
    man, stiff-jointed as a corpse,
Grotesquely erect, and old Aunt Stella her lips continually in
    motion, and old Jinny
Cross-legg'd having drawn up her ankles into her chair, nod-
    ding asleep. At length Aunt Stella
Ceased talking, none of the three stirred. Young Andrews
    backed into the wood and warily finishing
His circuit stood in the darkness under Tamar's window. The
    strong young tree to help him to it.
Still wore on its boughs her lamplight, then he climbed and
    set his hands on the sill, his feet on the ledge
Under it, and Tamar came to the window and took up the
    lamp to let him enter. Her face

White in the yellow lamp's glow, with sharp shadows under
    the eyes and a high look of joy
He had never seen there frightened him, and she said, "I have
    been sick, you know." "I heard," he answered,
"O Tamar, I have been lonely. We must let them know, we
    can't go on, my place is with you
When you most need me." "We will tell them to-night," she
    said, and kissed his mouth and called, "Lee, Lee,
Come. He has come." "What? Now," he said. "I have
    told Lee. I was sick, he was sorry for me, he is going
To camp to-morrow, he wants to see you and say good-by."
    Lee entered while she spoke and quietly
Held out his hand and Andrews took it. "Talk to each
    other," Tamar said, "I am very tired
And must lie down." Lee muttered "She's been awfully sick,
    it scared us, you were lucky, Bill Andrews,
Not to be here." "I didn't think so," he answered, "what
    was it, Lee?" "Well, it's all over," Lee said,
Shifting his feet, "I'm off to-morrow. I'm glad we're friends
    to say good-by. Be good to her, won't you."
And the other, "O God knows I will. All I can do. But of
    course . . . Lee . . . if they need me
She knows I won't beg off because I'm . . . married . . .
    maybe I'll see you over there." "O," said Tamar
Laughing, "you too?" and she sat up on the bed saying, "Lee:
    go and call father if he's able.
We ought to tell him, he ought to meet my—husband." "I'll
    see if he can," Lee answered, "he was unwell
To-day, and if he's in bed . . ." He left the room, then
    Tamar: "Look. Bring the lamp. What Lee did to me."
She opened the blue robe and bared her flank and thigh
    showing the long whip-mark. "I have a story.
You must see this to believe it." He turned giddy, the sweet
    slenderness
Dazzling him, and the lamp shook in his hand, for the sharp
    spasm of physical pain one feels

At sight of a wound shot up his entrails. That long welt of
red on the tender flesh, the blood-flecks
And tortured broken little channels of blood crossing it.
"Tamar, Tamar!" "Put down the lamp,
And when they come I'll tell you the story." "What shall I
do?" "Why, nothing, nothing. Poor boy," she said,
Pityingly, "I think you are too glad of your life to have come
Into this house, you are not hard enough, you are like my
mother, only stone or fire
Should marry into this house." Then he bewildered looking
at the blackened door-frame, "Why, yes,"
Laughed Tamar, "it is here, it has been here, the bride-
groom's here already. O Will I have suffered . . .
Things I daren't tell." "What do you mean, Tamar?" "Noth-
ing, I mustn't tell you, you are too high-tempered,
You would do something. Dear, there are things so wicked
that nothing you can do can make them better,
So horrible now they are done that even to touch or try to
mend or punish them is only to widen
Horror: like poking at a corpse in a pool. And father's old
and helpless." "Your father, Tamar?"
"And not to blame. I think he hardly even knew what
Lee——" "Lee?" "This much I'll tell you,
You have to know it . . . our love, your love and mine,
had . . . fruit, would have been fruitful, we were going
to have
A child, and I was happy and frightened, and it is dead. O
God, O God, O God, I wish
I too had been born too soon and died with the eyes unopened,
not a cry, darkness, darkness,
And to be hidden away. They did it to me; with other abuse,
worse violence." Meanwhile Lee Cauldwell
Finding his father with the two old women in the room down-
stairs, "Father," he said,
"Tamar was asking for you . . ." and Helen's voice through
old Aunt Stella answered, "She has enough,

[163]

Tell her she has enough."   "Aunt Stella," he said, "how long
     will you keep it up?   Our trouble's clearing,
Let your ghosts be."   "She has you and the other," she an-
     swered, "let me have this one.   Are we buzzards to quarrel
Over you dead, we ghosts?"   Then Lee turning his shoulder
     at her, "You must come up, father.
Do you remember the Andrews place that's up the valley?
     Young Andrews is up-stairs with Tamar,
He wants to marry her.   You know I have to go away to-
     morrow, remember?   and I'll go happier
To leave her . . . taken care of.   So you'll see him, father?"
     "Who is it?" asked the old man.   "The bridegroom,"
Said Helen's voice, "a bridegroom for your Tamar, and the
     priest will be fire and blood the witness,
And they will live together in a house where the mice are
     moles."   "Why do you plague me," he answered
Plaintively, and Lee: "Come, father," and he lifting his
     face, "I have prayed to the hills to come and cover me,
We are on the drop-off cliff of the world and dare not meet
     Him, I with two days to live, even I
Shall watch the ocean boiling and the sea curl up like paper
     in a fire and the dry bed
Crack to the bottom: I have good news for her, I will see her."
     "And I to tell her she may take
Two but not three," said Helen.   "Stay here, stay here, be
     quiet," Lee answered angrily, "can I take up
The whole menagerie, raving?"   He turned in the door and
     heard his father move behind him and said,
"If you come up, be quiet," and at the door up-stairs, "Father
     is tired and sick, he'll only
Speak to you, Andrews, and must go to bed; he's worried
     about my going away to-morrow.
This is Bill Andrews, father."   And Tamar coming to the door,
     "Let him come in, it's dark here,
No, bring him in.   Father come in.   What, shall the men that
     made your war suck up their millions,

Not I my three?" Then Andrews: "If Tamar is well enough
  to go to-night I will take her to-night.
You will be well when you are out of this house." "You hate
  it still," said Tamar. "He hates the house,"
She said to Lee, leading his eyes with the significance in hers
  to the blackened door-frame,
"Well, I will go with you to-morrow." And Lee, "Listen,
  Will Andrews, I heard from somebody
You know who set the fire here." "No, not that," he an-
  swered, "but I know other worse things
That have been done here." "Fire, fire," moaned the old man,
  "the fire of the Lord coming in judgment. Tamar,
It is well with us, be happy, He won't torture the wicked, He
  will rub them out and suddenly
With instant fire. We shall be nothing." "Come, Tamar,"
  Andrews cried, "to-night. I daren't leave you."
"For fear I ask her," said Lee. "You did it, then. You set
  the fire." "No, that's too idiot
A lie to answer," he said, "what do I know about your fires?
  I know something
Worse than arson. And saw the horrible new scar of a whip
Not to be paid—this way!" He felt the jerk of his arm
  striking
And his fist hitting the sharp edge of the jawbone, but yet
When Lee staggered and closed in with a groan,
Clutching him, fumbling for his throat, Will thought "What
  a fool
To make a nasty show of us before Tamar
And the others, why does he want to fight?" and indignantly
Pushed him off and struck twice, both fists, Lee dropped
And scrambled on hands and knees by the little table.
Then the old man cried, "We shall be nothing, nothing.
O but that's frightful."
And Will turning to Tamar saw such hatred
Wrinkle her face he felt a horrible surge
Of nausea in him, then with bare teeth she smiled at him
And he believed the hate was for her brother

[165]

And said, "Ah Tamar, come." Meanwhile the Helen
That spoke out of the lungs and ran in the nerves
Of old Aunt Stella caught the old man David Cauldwell
By the loose flapping sleeve and the lean arm,
Saying in a clotted amorous voice, "Come, David,
My brother, my lover, O honey come, she has no eyes for you,
She feasts on young men. But you to me, to me,
Are as beautiful as when we dared
Desperate pleasure, naked, ages ago,
In the room and by the sea." "Father," said Tamar,
"It is only an hour to the end, whom do you want
To-night? Stay here by me." "I was hunting for some-
     thing," said Lee Cauldwell,
"Here it is, here it is," and had the sheath-knife bared
And struck up from the floor, rising, the blade
Ripped cloth and skin along his enemy's belly
And the leather belt catching it deflected the point
Into the bowels, Andrews coughed and fell backward
And Lee falling across him stabbed at his throat
But struck too high and opened the right cheek,
The knife scraping on bone and teeth, then Tamar
In a sea-gull voice, "I dreamed it in his face,
I dreamed a T cut in his face——" "You and your dreams
Have done for us," Lee groaned answer. "Akh, all blood,
     blood.
What did you say to make him hit me?"

              Though it is not thought
That the dead intervene between the minds
And deeds of the living, that they are witnesses,
If anything of their spirits with any memory
Survive and not in prison, would seem as likely
As that an exile should look longingly home:
And the mist-face of that mother at the window
Wavering was but a witness, could but watch,
Neither prevent nor cause: no doubt there are many
Such watchers in the world: the same whom Andrews,

Stepping like a thief among the cypress clumps an hour before
Saw twist her hands and suddenly fling up both vaporous
   arms and sway out of the starlight,
She now was watching at the down-stairs window
Old Jinny alone in the room, and saw, as the dead see, the
   thoughts
More clearly than the cloth and skin; the child mind
In that old flesh gathered home on itself
In coils, laboring to warm a memory,
And worked on by an effluence, petulantly pushing away
The easier memories of its open time
Forty years back, power flowing from someone in that house
Belting it in, pressing it to its labor,
Making it shape in itself the memory of to-day's
Vision, the watcher saw it, how could she know it
Or know from whence? a girl naked, no, wrapped in fire,
Filmed in white sheets of fire. "Why, I'm like God,"
Old Jinny had said, "I see through walls," a girl
Naked though clothed in fire, and under the arms
Naked, no hair,—"Ah to be like her, to be like her, probably
Cloth, hair, burned off"; displaying herself before a wild old
   man
Who appeared part of the joy: "Ah, to be like her,
Fire is so sweet, they never let me play with it,
No one loves Jinny, wouldn't fire be a father
And hold her in his arms? Fire is so sweet,"
She hovered the hot lamp, "sweet fire, sweet light,"
She held a rag of paper above it, "O dear, dear fire,
Come and kiss Jinny, no one's looking,
Jinny's alone. Dear star, dear light, O lovely fire
Won't you come out, why is it turning black,
Ah come, Ah come, hug Jinny." The hungry beautiful bird
Hopped from its bird-cage to her. "I've got my star
Ah love, Ah love, and here's more paper
And a little of Jinny's dress, love, lovely light,
Jinny so loves you, Jinny's baby, Jinny's baby,

[167]

O," she screamed, "Oo, Oo, Oo," and ran to the window, folded
In a terrible wreath, and at her side the curtains
Danced into flame, and over her head; the gasp
That followed on a cry drew down a sword
Of flame to her lungs, pain ceased, and thinking "Father"
She dropped herself into the arms of the fire,
Huddling under the sill, and her spirit unprisoned
Filled all the room and felt a nuptial joy
In mixing with the bright and eager flame.
While from that blackened morsel on the floor
Fire spread to the wall and gnawed it through, and the window-glass
Crackling and tinkling a rush of south wind fed
The eagerness in the house.   They heard up-stairs
That brutal arch of crying, the quick crescendo,
The long drop and the following moan, Will Andrews
Struggled to rise and like a gopher-snake that a child
Has mashed the head of with a stone, he waggled
The blood-clot of his head over the floor
Gulping "You devils, you devils." Lee would have run down
But Tamar clung to him, the old man on his knees
Muttered to God, and old Aunt Stella
In no voice but her own screamed, screamed. Then fire
Was heard roaring, the door leaked threads of smoke,
Lee caught up Tamar in his arms and turned
To the window, the cypress-ladder, but his first step,
Blind, with the burden in his arms, the smoke in his eyes,
Trampled his murdered man on the floor who turning
Caught the other ankle and Lee went down and Tamar
So lovingly wound him that he could not rise
Till the house was full of its bright death; then Tamar:
"I will not let you take me. Go if you want."
He answered, "You devil, shall I go?" "You wouldn't stay!
Think of your black-eyed French girls." "We are on the edge of it," he answered,
"Tamar, be decent for a minute." "I have my three lovers

[168]

Here in one room, none of them will go out,
How can I help being happy? This old man
Has prayed the end of the world onto us all,
And which of you leaves me?" Then the old man: "O what
    mountain,
What mountain, what mountain?" And Lee, "Father. The
    window
We'll follow you." But he kneeling would not rise,
While the house moved and the floor sagged to the south
And old Aunt Stella through the opening door
Ran into the red and black, and did not scream
Any more; then Tamar, "Did you think you would go
Laughing through France?" And the old man, "Fierce, fierce
    light,
Have pity, Christ have pity, Christ have pity, Christ have
    pity,
Christ have pity,
Christ have pity . . ."
And Tamar with her back to the window embraced
Her brother, who struggled toward it, but the floor
Turned like a wheel.

    Grass grows where the flame flowered;
A hollowed lawn strewn with a few black stones
And the brick of broken chimneys; all about there
The old trees, some of them scarred with fire, endure the sea
    wind.

GALE IN APRIL

Intense and terrible beauty, how has our race with the frail
    naked nerves,
So little a craft swum down from its far launching?
Why now, only because the northwest blows and the headed
    grass billows,
Great seas jagging the west and on the granite
Blanching, the vessel is brimmed, this dancing play of the
    world is too much passion.
A gale in April so overfilling the spirit,
Though his ribs were thick as the earth's, arches of moun-
    tain, how shall one dare to live,
Though his blood were like the earth's rivers and his flesh
    iron,
How shall one dare to live? One is born strong, how do the
    weak endure it?
The strong lean upon death as on a rock,
After eighty years there is shelter and the naked nerves shall
    be covered with deep quietness,
O beauty of things go on, go on, O torture
Of intense joy I have lasted out my time, I have thanked God
    and finished,
Roots of millennial trees fold me in the darkness,
Northwest wind shake their tops, not to the root, not to the
    root, I have passed
From beauty to the other beauty, peace, the night splendor.

MAL PASO BRIDGE

1

Under the lovely Santa Lucian hills
Between the steep-up slopes and storm-piled sea's
Green turbulence I rode northward, beneath
Armies of cloud on the headlands. Garapatas
Passed, over Soberanes Canyon hung
A Sierran condor on spread sails, the storm
Moved him not, the massed body of heaven above him
Moved and he solitary in the great wind
That slighter wings could not endure abode.
Under Mal Paso bridge the long-maned sea-waves
Beat up into the stream, on the other bank
A woman with a little child was standing,
Her daughter three years old, the woman's face
Though it seemed white against the storm was brown,
Her body and face I thought were beautiful,
Her eyes and hair were stormier than the cloud,
I trembled when she turned her eyes upon me.
Turbulent loveliness did you know then,
Or only a fortnight later the full storm
Of male desire? You are the shallow creek-mouth
The surf of all my seas converged upon.
Were I that mountain vulture, solitary
And unmoved under the rush of monstrous heavens,
You would have been the arrow and brought me down.
But when I bought you with a smile and whispers
And secret gifts of wine then the arrow was blunted.

2

This is the year when young men cannot guess
From night to night what bed they'll sleep in.
But I in yours dark beauty of new desire,
Yours under Santa Lucian hills
Near the rough water; but beyond that nor moon
Nor guess candles the remnant nights.
Therefore I swore to drink wine while I could,
Love where I pleased, and feed my eyes
With Santa Lucian sea-beauty, and moreover
To shear the rhyme-tassels from verse.

3

No doubt God kept the cows away
To let the grass grow long and dry
Under the white-oak up the canyon.

And frightened with a noise of dogs
Those moonlighters the misty deer,
He made the bed, he kept it sacred.

O keep it hidden and holy still,
Let nothing, bird nor beast nor man,
Touch our joy's chamber under the oaktree.

4

Iron is the world's want now,
The desire of the nations adventurous iron
Running ahead in the front of the violence,
And war-making steel the hard-visaged adventurer.

Let us give two nights to love
And one to the beautiful goodness of wine,
Stars we will gather you, hills you shall dance with us
To meet the grave brows of the morning high-heartedly.

[172]

5

The war-cruisers well-steerable and steel-belted
Traversing the prone sea
From eloquent round mouths in their mailed towers
Profess a metal language
Beyond the remote horizon ponderously
Significant; the broad storm-cloud
Can kill far off with hazardous quick-flaming
And crooked spears; the Sierras
Have white and roaring lances that they fling
When rose-awakening May
Fondles them, blue-eyed temptress; but I that walk
Ill-armed this dangerous earth
Have only verse, a light weapon, that leaves
In the wound seeds of live fire.

6

In dream I hunted the latest vessel of the old desire
Across an ancient foreign city
Through coiling streets, a city at war, for every moment
Enemy fire and metal death
Dropped messages from the doubtful twilight; still I sought,
But found not whom I sought, she eluded
Desire and death also. I stood before the sculptured
Gateway of an old dingy house.
My father who is dead stood in the door and beckoned,
And on the granite of the lintel
A serpent dragged its polished body, the color of stone.
. . . It will be years before I can enter.

7

Dark pearl, rose of the hills, star of the sea,
Dark star, angel of hell, I am mad for your body,
I am sick for the smell of your hair, I have burning for heart
And the sun for my hatred, and you.

Slim deer grazing at night knew that you lied.
Gray gulls gossip about us, they scream in the fountains
Of the surf, "He believed in her beauty, he is fooled like a
  boy
Who will spaniel a smile and a braid."

8

White bird beating between the hilltops
Rises the dawn at the head of the valley,
The hush of the stars.
The redwoods shake their columns of shadow,
Deep in darkness whisper the waters
An adorable word.
Through the cool calm and the secret twilight
Silver-foreheaded, saintly, a maiden,
Wonderfully move
Light, and the waters nightlong wakeful
Whenever we listened, and the sacred hilltops
Whitening in heaven.

THE COAST-RANGE CHRIST

I

Peace O'Farrell, the Carmel farmer's wife, was sorrowful day
    and night,
Found no joy in being young and could have wished the
    yellow hair white.
What is youth for but to spill it with joy at the altar-foot
    of life?
What right has a wild old man in the useless beauty of a
    young wife?
David Carrow forded the river, a youth with wide and simple
    eyes,
To distinguish the strained face, pools in a rock reflecting
    skies.
"Are you looking for your father's horses David, that strayed
    this way?
Jamie sicked the collie on them to stop them nosing the
    stacked hay.
They ran up and crossed the bridge, they'll be at the gate
    when you get home.
David you might stay and talk to me for a minute since
    you've come.
I'm so lonely these days, Jamie hates me, I'll leave him when
    I can.
Christian David, tell me would that be wicked?" "You
    mustn't rob a man."
"Rob his hayfield of a squirrel, it's likely he'd mind, he's
    tired of me now.
Rob his orchard of a little ripe apple he leaves to rot on the
    bough."

[175]

"Peace, I'm sorry," David said.   Peace watched the muscles
in his cheek

Work, for he felt ashamed; she flung restraint to the wind
thinking him weak.

David drew from her hot arms but the hot soft kiss was like
a devil

Following him across the shoal though he prayed to be de-
livered from evil;

Though he'd harder cattle to herd, young men were being
conscripted now

Up to the rage of nations, not for a coward's reason he dared
not go;

Dreamer of mystical brotherhood he had built to music a
mountain of faith

Over desperate Golgotha rock and found a star to follow to
death.

II

Walking in his father's field when shadows grew long and
leaned toward night

David felt the law and prison reach out for him, he prayed
for a light.

Waking in his bed when shadows began to flock to the water-
side

David fancied men were come to take him and prayed to
Christ his guide.

"Lord our love and savior lead me, make me worthy to suffer
like you

At men's hands and in their walls, it will be hard, it is little
to do.

But last night when I was walking in the field, and in the
night

While I slept, a voice came and a dream Lord, so I cry for
a light.

For it said to hide in the hills, I thought that it was your
voice Dear.

But to hide seems wrong, I am ready to suffer now, I cannot
    see clear.
Then my dream, I stood in the hills, in the deep woods of the
    hills, I saw
You, Dear, walking on Potrero Hill and wept with wonder
    and awe."
David prayed, his own soul crying to him to escape to the
    hills and hide.
Secretly enthroned his own soul answered the prayer, that
    God his guide.

III

Where the Carmel River leans upon its sand-bar in love with
    the waves,
And the old Franciscan churchyard feels the wild gourd fin-
    ger its graves
While the weed-roots eat the chalk-stone walls, the O'Farrell
    farmlands lay.
All the country is shot with the endless treasure-stories of
    Monterey.
Tales of the lost Spanish mine the Indians know of up in
    the hill,
Where their forefathers were whipped like cattle, they keep
    the secret still.
Stories of brigands' loot and priests' hoards buried between
    a night and a day;
Tales of tall ships bulging with sterling silver and mutiny
    beached in the bay.
Tales that focussed on O'Farrell's own farmland, the core of
    the coast domain
Granted the mendicants of St. Francis by the majesty of
    Spain.
In O'Farrell's potato-field the plow-iron yielded convert
    bones,
Though his mole-plow never had cut to treasure, but the
    farmer had once

Saved a grizzled Indian's life when the river was up and
his horse went down,
Hauled him through the tawny freshet tearing the alders
tempest-blown.
With no word of thanks the old man went dripping up hill
and disappeared;
Ten days later he returned and squatted all day in the stable
yard,
Slept in the loft straw at night and in the morning said he'd
bid
Silver for life: when the priests were hunted out of the Mis-
sion church they hid
Deep their hoard, O'Farrell dig here and find old silver as
cheap as salt,
Candlesticks and cups and ingots rocked-in at night in the
rich vault.
No, he had better work to mind, the winter plows and the
summer reaping;
But years after, an autumn evening while he lay between
waking and sleeping
Came a voice on the valley-wind "O'Farrell dig here." He
smiled and slept.
In a dream his mother came, her hair was earthy and wet and
she wept.
There was silver at her throat, earth-tarnished now for thirty
years.
When he waked he thought it wise to dig, he was so moved
by her tears.
At twelve feet he tapped a tunnel underground but it led to
nothing.
Nearer to the river he sunk another shaft, with longing and
loathing.
Not for need of the white metal, the plows were turning up
gold that year,
He was longing to withdraw from concealment . . . to lift
into the air . . .

Something . . . that white child of the earth . . . to violate
the secrets of earth.
Said he was digging a new well, blasphemed when water bub-
bled forth.
Toiled with long-forgotten hankering, baby fingers never at
rest
Fumbling for a silver trinket that used to swing in the
mother's breast.
Sapping at the man's grown nerves the helpless baby's fear
and desire,
Like a crystal fault in granite, unseen till the lintel cracks,
or a fire
Sown in harbor in a ship's hold where it smoulders seven days
With no smoke and then the lonely midmost ocean beholds
the blaze.
Mother's love eclipsed the dues of the living, itself in its
darkness hid,
Obscure moon of the dead; the secret child within him ruled
what he did.
Tore at his sleep and tortured him, and let his hired Swiss
run the farm
While he credited crazy symbols, for omens flock as the vul-
tures swarm
Over carrion, to shadow the shaky-nerved. . . . Peace also
had singular dreams,
Swam in a pool of darting serpents, or played in a novel-
ist's chariot-games,
Under thousands of men's eyes round the high stone altars
and theater-courses,
Scaled with plates of blazing silver, guiding a galloping hur-
ricane of horses.

IV

Hicks, the sheriff's man drove up to the door and switched off
his machine.
"How do you do, Mrs. O'Farrell?" "Why, Sherman Hicks,
is it you? Come in."

"Just on business, Peace. We used to think there was better than that between us.

Have you seen Dave Carrow around, they want him over there in Salinas."

"David—what do you want David for?" "The draft-board wants him, Peace.

Called him and he didn't show up, his people don't know where he is,

Least they say they don't." "I don't know either, I haven't seen him in weeks.

David a coward and slacker, I hope you catch him." "Likely we will," said Hicks.

"I was talking to Walt Vogel, he says he's watched the old woman crawl

Up the hillside when the sun went down with a bundle wrapped in a shawl."

"Sanctified young puppy," said Peace, "that yellow streak is certain to show.

Once he tried to kiss me, the crazy boy; I never liked him though;

Christian David." "Do boys often try?" "Jamie's away so much,

Digging his new wells—No! Sherman." "God, Peace you're a sweet girl to touch."

"Sherman, I'm half crazy myself, but let it be, it's over now.

Hope you catch your slacker, if I hear about him I'll let you know."

V

Peace dreamed marvelously all night and Carmel Mission the desolate church

Grown much larger and more lovely and belted with a shining porch

Of enormous pillars blazed with rosy light, the whole beauty was hers,

All her blood went wild to feel the aisles fill up with worshipers.

Indians and all sorts of men, and women with sheer silk
bridal veils,
Bold vaqueros with broad spurs and bandit captains out of
old tales.
Soldiers too, thousands of soldiers, bayonet-carriers, beautiful
killers,
Tall Americans and short Frenchmen shouldering the crowd
in the shadow of the pillars.
First the worshipers adored the small star-window over the
door,
While the door moved eagerly wide for the entrance of multi-
tudes more and more.
Then the sweet silver and terrible bells rang out wild wel-
come and swayed the domed steeple,
While the sucking wings of the doorway pulsed and quivered
for the entrance of people.
Next the multitude adored the crucifix over the high stone
altar,
There a serpent for Christ was hanging, the whole crowd
worshiped and did not falter.
Wild choirs of boys' voices pealed, in unison all the roof-tiles
rang,
All the rafters gave a silver noise and all the columns sang.
Sepulchered saints beneath the altar began to sing for Peace
and to call.
She—her vestment silks were torn and she would be shamed
before them all.
Her the crowd awaited, now it was crying her name, it howled
like a wolf,
Horrible fears ran blind through her body, a luxury of shame,
what hiding, what gulf?
Suddenly out of a smell of ferns and streams, out of the quiet
hill-mist,
David came and clasped her shoulder, "Come with me Peace,
we will see Christ."
Though her body was naked he did not see nor mind, her
mouth was chill

[181]

With sweet water and canyon streams, and death it seemed,
   in the sleep of the hill.
When the gates of the east were widened, the wan stars
   gathered home their gleams,
Golden-haired the gorgeous day came out of the valley to kill
   dreams.

VI

Peace had left the work to the servant after the noon meal
   was done,
When the hateful hour had passed and her husband and the
   men were gone.
Peace went up to her own room and watched from the win-
   dows west and south
Sea-gulls weave a windy storm-dance over the shore at the
   Carmel mouth.
Gulls by thousands flying the south wind, two swarms like
   columns slender and far
Towering from the Carmel sand-beach and spiring above the
   Carmel bar.
Columns curving on the wind and rootless near the water;
   and higher
Up the beautiful coast-range hills were columns of smoke and
   crescents of fire.
Where the ranchers fired their hill-fields, they felt the hurry
   of wind from the south,
Hoped the waited rain would come, they were clearing the
   pastures for new growth.
All the hills were glassy clear, the yellow slopes and the trees
   beyond
Like a picture under glass or like the moss in a quiet pond.
Peace began to tremble greatly, and found in a drawer, done
   in old cloth,
Field-glasses, and focused them to her eyes and felt the
   heights of the south.
Homesick for the forest, and full of hatred she thought for
   David, turning

To the quiet slopes on the right, away from the ridge where
fires were burning.
Searching pines and bushes of sage and lupine, the deer-
paths and rabbit-runs,
Cattle-paths, and the dim wheel-tracks up from Carrow's
farm, and once
While she watched a shadow a man's form passed in the
forest, the glasses shaking
Split the vision, her arms and eyes were so weary and all her
body was aching.
But at sundown she saw a woman, and knew it was David's
mother, steal
Up the cow-path with a bundle wrapped in a shawl, and up
the hill.
Hands shook and breath shortened again, the woman wound
back and forth from sight,
Stood by a tree, returned without the bundle through the
gathering night.
"Ah, my Christian Davie, blue-eyed forest coyote, caught I
say, caught.
Poor old mother thinking her boy hungry, it's more than food
you've brought.
Better have left him poison mother, a traitor and coward, far
better have touched
Twenty-two years ago the heavy nipple with strychnine when
the young lips clutched.
Now he'll rot his shame in prison." Peace, laughing and
laying the glasses down,
Called up Sherman Hicks, the sheriff's deputy, on the tele-
phone;
Told him what she'd seen, "And you," she said, "drive up by
the valley road,
Leave your car and climb the ridge, we'll catch our fox when
he comes for his food.
You must climb the ridge, I'll call one of the farmhands and
ride by the west,

David will be caught between us before we meet on the hill crest.

There's no underbrush to hide in, only a few pines standing alone.

Quietly Sherman, very quietly. No lights, we'll have the full of the moon."

Hicks was laughing to himself to find so eager a volunteer.

"Better let me walk in the hills and you be safe in bed, my dear.

Ain't good sense for a pretty woman to poke about in the woods at night.

There's a south wind blowing up clouds and there'll be precious little light,

Peace, from that full moon of yours to see with an hour or so.

Then, besides, your husband mightn't like it." "No," answered Peace, "I'll go.

Better to ride in the dark hills than dream of the horrors all night long.

Trust me to take care of myself, I'll take my automatic along."

Peace went out and found her husband fetching a lantern from the shed.

"Jamie, won't you come with me, I've got to go for a ride," Peace said.

"Going to help the sheriff's deputy catch a slacker up in the wood.

David Carrow's dodging the draft, I saw his mother taking him food.

I can help, it's war-time, Jamie, each one of us must help as we're able."

But he answered, "I've got to fetch another lantern out of the stable.

For I'm going to work all night, it'll rain before to-morrow night.

There's a south wind blowing up rain, I've got to work by lantern light.

Rain will come the river'll flood, the rain will wash the dirt
  like salt,
But I've struck the second tunnel running down to the rich
  vault.
I've been digging in a dirt of dead men's bones for seven or
  eight weeks,
Sunk a shaft and run a drift, and you can ride with Sherman
  Hicks.
Ride and be damned, it's nothing to me." "But, Jamie dear,
  if you won't come
Let me have George or Johnny or Frank to see me safe and
  bring me home."
"No, I'll need their help to cut the sand-bar, you can't have
  one of the men,
For I'll want them all in the morning if the floodwaters
  begin."

VII

On the hills were crescents of fire that crackled and spurted
  blood-red light,
Over the hills the patient moon was spilling silver down the
  night.
Peace rode high in the pines and James her husband dug his
  pit in the earth,
Burning to rake old riches from concealment and bring the
  earth's child to birth.
Amorously piercing the impure depth, the prone breast lulled
  by the night.
Plowing a channel for his dream with shovel and pick by
  lantern light.
Peace rode up in the open pinewood, clouds were pushed up
  over the moon,
Patches of light, patches of dark, on the open hill slope
  plunging and strewn.
In a patch of shadow her pony shied, a boy said tender-
  voiced:

"I was waiting for you up here, come with me, Peace, we will
see Christ."
"We'll see Sherman Hicks, the deputy-sheriff, that's the man
we must see.
David, you're a fool to have run away from the fighting;
and, David, from me.
When I kissed you on your mouth, have you forgotten,
David?" "Not yet.
But in jail I'll soon forget and here in the hills I'd soon
forget.
It was nothing, Peace. So you've come up to catch me?"
"How can I know?
But to own you body and soul. I can give you up, I can let
you go.
God, it's pleasant, David, to possess you; to own a man like
a horse.
This one moment you're all mine, I can give you up to prison
or worse,
I can set you free of the hills, dear, I can do better than let
you go,
Find you money and make you a way and over the border
to Mexico.
Choose, you'll kiss me, David?" "I'll do more, O Peace, you
homing dove,
Lovely and perfect messenger, come with me, Peace, we will
see love.
It was hurting here in my brain, in the nights I dreamed of
you alone,
When I ought to have dreamed of Jesus Christ the other
adorable one.
I was angry at you, Peace, for drawing me down from the
promised desire,
Now I see that God was at work and both of us fagots for
that fire:
Let your pony graze, come down the gulch with me, Peace,
till the men are gone.

[186]

God has sworn me promises. O Peace, your love and Christ's
   are one."
"You would hurt me, David." "O we are going to the fire,
   the fire of the world
Ending, heaven beginning, spirits set loose, the seas burned,
   the stars hurled.
Love me, Peace. I love you. That is Christ. I love you,
   I love you, Peace.
All the world is slipping to cinders about us and love is all
   that there is,
Come, my Peace, come Peace." "Ah, but you'd hurt me,
   David." "I will not touch
Even your hair's tip with my lips, I love you too much, I love
   you too much."
Marvelous sorcery of the night, the splintered moon-gleams,
   the south wind gushing,
Pines, the sky so near, the fires, the high withdrawal, the
   south wind pushing.
Peace swung down from the saddle, "We both are crazy,
   David. Come. You and I."
Down the gulch they lay in a shadow and heard the sheriff's
   man go by.
Heard the horse puff, the man pause; and heard him catch
   the horse, and stand still.
Heard the pumping of their blood and the south wind pouring
   across the hill.
After enormous intervals the man called once or twice, the
   south
Washed his voice down the dark slope. Peace carried David's
   hand to her mouth.
Now the moon was gone, the hill-fold hid the fires, no stars,
   no light.
Peace had whipped her arms around David's neck. The man
   rode by in the night.
David wished to rise. "Hush, he'll comb all the hill, there's
   no good way

But lie still and wait, against the sky he'd see us, black against gray.

Sweetheart, rest on me," she said. "How can I rest, we have Christ to find."

"Sweetheart, rest on me in this secret harbor out of the beating wind."

"Peace, when you came up to catch me then you were not betraying me." "Hush.

Where is Christ? but love grows here on the hill, wild, wild, God's grape to crush.

Sent by God, you said I was. A wild grape, a wild gift in the dark.

Storm to hide us. When dawn comes if you hate me kill me at the first spark."

Now the storm grew heavy with rain, the burdened south wind let big drops fall.

Peace could feel her flesh move at their touch, her mind felt nothing at all

Of the storm, but only a confused fire, her lips felt David's lips

In the sensuous gatherings of the wind and the night, in the world's eclipse.

Down below the big drops thudded on fresh earth, in the valley below

Where that silver-covetous mole was burrowing by the river's flow

In his tunnel with his lanterns; and westward the horizontal drift

Skimmed the ocean, pelting the waves sidewise under the weather's lift.

Eastward where the greedy brush-fires bent under the buffeting wind

Hissed the rain, red steam poured up the night, the coals blackened, went blind.

But far eastward under another rain there was metal raining too,

[188]

Fire and metal, and men laboring and fighting in a filth of
mud like glue.

Peace was pasturing in the rain on the little field of her
despair,

Eating the reckless heart of joy with lips like fire through
the loosened hair.

"David. Ah. Ah. Dearest. Kill me, kill me now; how
can I live

All the coming years?" In a moment David prayed, "God,
God, forgive

Me this woman's pitiful fool." He moaned, he struck her
mouth and her throat's

Curve, she screamed and ripped her pistol from its case and
fired three shots.

Up the hill came a cry in answer. Peace ran to the hoof-
beats. "Help, Sherman. Ride. Ride!

Sherman. Kill the beast. He dragged me from the saddle.
He struck me, he tried . . ."

"Which way did he run?" "Up there, up hill." The man
spurred, the horse went down,

Winded from the slope, tripped in a gopher-burrow. "God
damn it, I'm thrown."

He was cursing the rain and the horse, the hills, the darkness,
the hurt in his side.

Peace came and he grumbled, "Sorry, Peace. He's out, no
good to ride,

Fetlock snapped, your pony. We can't do more to-night.
I'll take you home.

But I'll catch that running devil, by God, if it takes till
kingdom come."

"Sherman, you're not hurt?" "No, did he hurt you, Peace?"
"He struck me. . . . No.

And I'm not going home, not till we get him, Sherman; I
say I won't go."

"O you're plucky, Peace." "I think I hit him once, yes the
first shot.

Beast. The filthy beast. The filthy beast. He struck my
mouth and my throat."

"Hell's too sweet for these damned runaway cowards, the
army'll deal them worse,"

Sherman answered, fumbling at wet buckles, unbridling the
fallen horse.

Furiously the rain came down, in a moment the gully they
were in

Flowed, a distant lightning flash drew cataracts on the hill
and the lean

Pine-trees arched in the flurry of weather. Peace began
screaming, "Rain, dear rain,

Poison his bullet wound I made, storm break his bones, blind
him with pain.

Lightning scald his eyes but never kill him." Her voice broke
and went wild,

Back her head snapped and she screamed like a beast and
choked and sobbed like a child.

Sherman begged her to be quiet, then shook her with his
hands, and he heard

Someone crying not far away, and panting up hill, and the
storm poured.

"Who is there, who is it?" he said. Peace laughed, "The old
mother of the dog.

Mother, have you brought him more food, he won't eat it, I
fed him a lead slug."

Sherman's flashlight played across the rain-lines on a gray
form they veiled,

Streaming soaked gray hair and a gray sick face and gray
lips gasping, "Killed?"

"No. He's got away from us. You're his mother." "David's
mother, yes, yes,"

Breathed the old woman blinking at the light and panting.
Then suddenly Peace

Laughed, "My God, to think that such a withered old nut-
shell had such meat.

Mother, have you brought him more food, he won't eat it, I
gave him lead to eat."
"Killed? She means he's dead." Hicks answered, "No,
ma'am, he's got away up the hill."
Peace cried out, "Your milk was too weak, old poisoner; he'll
rot in a prison, he will."
Hicks said, "Will you help me with the lady, ma'am; she's
clean off her head.
Had a bad fall on the hill, her horse fell, busted its leg," he
said.
"Broke his leg—my boy?" "No, no, the horse did, the horse
fell, the lady's hurt."
"O poor Mrs. O'Farrell, it's you; do come, dear." "You,
mother of dirt,"
Mumbled Peace, "I'll spit on you if you touch me. Wet hag
don't dare," she screamed.
So the three stood gazing. Gray in the vault of the rain
the flashlight gleamed.
Suddenly Peace straightened and fell, and Sherman lifted her
and said,
"Mrs. Carrow, we must take her to your house; we must get
her to bed."
Down the hill they toiled together, stumbling over pine-roots
and stones;
Hundred-gurgling water shuttered from their ears the hurt
horse's groans.

VIII

David lay on the torrent hillside and tore at a flesh-wound
in his thigh,
Drenched his finger-nails in the running blood praying God
to make him die.
Down in the valley James O'Farrell deepened his empty mine
in vain;
Down the dirt-wall of the shaft a serpent rivulet of the rain
Crawled, the lanterns gave it two red eyes. He dug in the
fume and dust

With religious fear, he found each lump of earth an omen to
trust,
Felt in every bit of gravel or quartz-brilliant or mica flake
Memories of some dream, and a promise sacred for a prayer's
sake.
There were two men bound for death, one lay on the hill and
tore his wound,
One was tearing at the deep breast of his mother, both were
death-bound.
Over all the valley and hill and over the black woods and
black waves
Poured the solid waters of the permanent rain from clouds
like caves.
From the mossed pines at Point Pinos south to the Big Sur
redwood groves
Trees were trembling with delight and dreaming roots remem-
bered their loves.
Seeds began to swell in their dreams and omens filled the
streaming earth,
Omens of lifting from concealment . . . of raising in the air
. . . of bringing to birth . . .
Stirrings of the secret force that gathers itself under the
ground
To make signals in the splendid light of day when the year
turns round.
David prayed, "I have soiled myself to the bone, I am blacker
than hell and this night,
Let my body that sinned be punished, kill me and clean me,
bleed me all white,
Draw my spirit out of this sheath of death, the damnation of
proud hope
Tripped me while I ran in the hills, dear God this dirt be
covered up,
Buried under, damned and blotted down in the dirty breast
of the earth.
Draw my spirit from hiding, lift it up in the air, God; O draw
it forth.

To be least and lowest in heaven, and a servant of the happy
and sweet
Faithful in some little thing that see no higher than to your
feet.
For I held your promise, O God the son of God to see you
a traitor and fool.
Crazy with pride, and the first and least temptation left me
whole,
There is no one such a fool, no traitor so little tempted, not
one,
Nowhere such a vessel and beast of weakness, nowhere under
the sun.
No one, nowhere," droned his despair; flowing blood enfeebled
it so he fell
Fast asleep in the waves of rain, in darkness like the valley
of hell.
Dreamless sleep like heavy and deep waters covered his head,
but when
Earth turned dawnward a weak dream swam over him, he
seemed a child again.
Playing and wading along the sea-beach he found a cave
among the rocks,
Where he lay to watch his father plowing the field above,
while flocks
Of white sea-birds hovered plowman and horses and the
happy and opened earth.
He was hidden, he would delight in the cave, nothing should
coax him forth.
David slept on the torrent hillside and James O'Farrell went
fast asleep
Over his tools in the valley tunnel, a sleep like lead or heavy
and deep
Waters covered his tired head, the lanterns flared and they
died, but when
Earth turned dawnward a dream swam down the darkness,
he seemed a child again.
Saw the yellow Ohio sucking its low shores under dim trees;

He was fishing from the bank, his sister barefoot to the lean
    knees
Helped him when the line was tangled on a snag, then she
    went down
Among quicksands, the quicksands murmured, "I am your
    mother, I am your own
Mother and sister, prod me with your fishing-pole, we are
    down here,
Waiting to be weighed from concealment . . . to be lifted in
    the wild air . . ."

IX

Peace O'Farrell awoke in the Carrows' empty farmhouse and
    seemed to know
Instantly in the darkness all that had been done night hours
    ago.
David's mother had tenderly undressed her and rubbed her
    skin and her hair
With warm towels, and heated flat-irons for her feet so ice-
    cold they were.
Tended her like an old nurse and soothed her moans and
    stroked her head,
Given her some hot drink she would not swallow, and tucked
    her in David's bed.
Peace remembered where her clothes were hung though she
    had been senseless then.
First she thought she must off the old woman's night-dress,
    though it was laundered clean
Still it was that old woman's; Peace felt purer when it lay
    on the floor.
Warm from bed she felt no cold at all; but the planks cried,
    and the door
Violently cracked its hinges, and if she should knock a chair
    in the little hall
All the house would be up with lights and she would be
    shamed before them all.

Lights, why the hall was dizzy with light. Peace stood like
    iron in the low door,
Like a wild beast cornered, too proud to hide her body. "I
    will hide it no more,"
Moved her thought, "I have hid my womanhood too long,
    from myself even.
Was it indeed so shameful?" Low in the west, more on the
    sea than in heaven
Rolled the broad moon, all the rain was banished, the clouds
    were gone in the west,
Level through the window played the splendor and lay like
    flame on her breast.
Native of the light she burned on the oblong blackness all
    silver and flame,
Female and not veiled, though eyes had been there to see her
    she could have felt shame
No more than a cloudless mountain the low dawn fountains
    up light to seek,
When the cedar shadows are upright like the cedars on the
    slope to the peak.
She stole down the moonlit stair and found her clothes on
    chairs by the hearth.
No one stirred in any chamber, and the door was not locked,
    and she stole forth
Leaving to its ghosts an empty house, and followed the
    shadows up
Eastward, with the wash of the lit sea behind, and ahead the
    long slope.

X

James O'Farrell awoke and found himself in fear in the dark
    of the womb,
Smothered in a horror of smelling earth in the musky mother
    tomb.
Pressed by mass and brutal tons and buried out of sight and
    of mind,

Stench of dead earth and starved lights, concealed and lost,
   buried and blind.
Like a drowned man in mid-ocean or like a dead man in the
   mid-heart
Of a public graveyard, caverned with thousands, a communist
   people of dirt.
Nothing pure or erect or private, no separate honor, no in-
   scribed stones,
But the liquids of each rotting body run through on a brother's
   bones.
David Carrow awoke on the hill in the wonderful pure and
   honey-sweet
Shining of the moon in the west, and the valley was like a
   lake at his feet.
Night was only a dreamed hell, and the hurt in his thigh was
   like the scar
Where a soldier gored the side of God, the flesh of the morn-
   ing star.
Strength of the human soul to suffer or sin to its dream's
   uttermost
And forget it all in an hour and fling at the stars like a young
   hawk loosed.
James O'Farrell broke through his dream and crawled along
   the drift to the shaft,
Where a phantom pallor of twice-reflected moonlight silently
   laughed,
Swimming on a puddle below the minehead, and up the ladder
   a skin
Of green starless cloudless sky, and a falling, the river was
   running in.
Seen from the top ladder-steps the valley was all a lake from
   the south,
White and silent mirror of moonlight backing up from the
   sand-barred mouth,
Beautiful and a death of hope. "Why should I dig again,"
   he said.

"You are too strong old mother, you have damned me with
  signs and lies, you hide your dead.
All the pretty promises broken, you liar.   You'd have kept
  me and choked me down there.
Suck your own dirt animal maw, I will not go down, I will
  die in the air."
While the water lapped his feet he kicked the loose earth
  over the rim,
Watched the eager cataract eat the heaps, and the banks
  bulge down and brim.
There at the cataract end of life he stood and looked at the
  hill slope,
Where there were height, and splendid inclines of spacious
  moonlight, and a lifting hope.
Hope the ghost of hope reached back for a hold on life, like
  the talking dead,
Shells of extinct men, the larvæ and masks that hover a
  medium's head.
"I will go up in the hills," he said, "and find the sun in the
  hills, and there
Work this body from concealment and weigh it up high in
  the wild air . . ."
Walking like a stone-faced sleepwalker, his feet not feeling
  the earth,
With the moon-gleam in his white eyes, he caught a horse and
  looped the girth,
Took a hackamore along besides the bridle, and as he rode
Worked a knot in the rough horse-hair.   From the bridge he
  saw the moonlit flood
Plating half his pasture-land with pure sheet silver, and half
  a mile down
Breakers flung black handfuls above the bar across the sea-
  faring moon.

XI

Peace O'Farrell strained up the slope and heard a sobbing
  under a pine.

"What are you doing here, gray mother?" "My boy. Whatever he's done he's mine.
God, dear God for the little boy that used to look into my face,
With his hands holding my finger and his body against my old knees.
In the milky days before they made a war, when my boy was my own,
When he wanted no woman but me and Christ and the war could let him alone.
Sherman Hicks went out the door when the rain was done in the moonlight shine,
And I followed him up the cow-path and fell down against a pine.
David's father came and passed me, and raving mad because of the stain
David tried to do to you, Mrs. O'Farrell, in the sickness of his brain."
"Sick, I know he's sick," Peace answered, "and sick enough and ready to die.
Show me which way Sherman went, and I'll beg off for your baby, I'll try.
Tell me which way Sherman went, you sack of bones get up if you can.
I'll take after Sherman Hicks and you must catch your crazy old man."
"Sweetheart," mumbled the old creature, "he went by the left by the broken tree,
But it's no use knocking the darkness now the moon's gone down in the sea."
Peace went up the solid darkness and heard the mother stumble behind.
Sherman clambered near the height, the west was blackened, the night blind.
James O'Farrell rode up the under-slope, fumbling the hackamore still.

David Carrow stood on the height and there were six came up
the hill.
Three were men and two were women, the sixth was neither
man nor woman,
He was higher and lovelier than the pine-tops, and human
and not human.
He was a shining out of the east before the star that kills the
night,
Like a walking tower on the ridge between the hilltops, a
tower of light.
Peace O'Farrell believed he was the dawn, and by the light
of him saw
David kneel on the lonely hilltop, waving his arms with won-
der and awe.
And saw Sherman walking through a bush, dazzled and black
in the shine,
And saw risings at the sky, and pine-stumps move on the
mountain line.
David wept, his weakness and tears and pain were the serv-
ants of delight,
In the sudden apocalypse of love, the splitting asunder of
night.
Darkness was torn both ways like a cloth and cast on the
earth like a sheet;
David dared not look at the face for the fiery lightning of
the feet.
Wild choirs of boys' voices and of men's and women's wan-
dered the mountain,
Music poured along the ridge and a pointed fire of flutes like
a fountain
Jetted from the peak and joined the swimming stars, the
stars sang chime,
Carollers ranged the breaking night for it was near the
Christmas time.

CHOROS

God was a hawk in the glow of the morning, a bee in the
    rose that has stars for her petals,
The far lights felt him, the first-born lamps
Spun from the brush of his wings when he bathed in the
    splendor of a firmament men's eyes never imaged,
Exulting in the beauty of things, a free eagle.
But love drew him dustward, for love's sake he stooped, like
    a lover came God with a garland of suns
In his locks and the wild wine freedom on his lips
To the earth and the arms of a Jewess, and to house with a
    tribe of tame serpents in the handmaiden planet
Of a least of the stars—the descent of the lover.

ANTICHOROS

You mountains of Asia a vain tale came to us once in old days
    when we tasted the sunlight,
It was said that a Savior inherited the earth.
That his footsteps from Syria were fruitful and the honey of
    his lips from Samaria made beautiful the nations
With powerful obedience and the peoples with peace.
Gray mountains of Asia we have come to the end of that
    dream, when we touched it the iris-tinted
Bubble was a froth-work of blood and of fire.

David saw the hearts of men in the east, in Europe and Asia
    too,
And his own was like a singing breaking glass, or a globe of
    dew.

[200]

Peace O'Farrell saw little of these things, she only felt she
    must save
David, and she hasted and caught Sherman's hand, and the
    kiss that she gave
Was no sister of Iscariot's. "Why do you think I went on
    the height,
Sherman dear, and risked myself in the night for nothing and
    again in the night?
Was it to catch your slacker, what do I want with that, it
    was all for you.
It was hard to find a chance, those married eyes can see me
    through.
Think I'll make another chance if this one doesn't win me a
    kiss?"
He was manageable, this man. And David was left to his
    happiness.

CHOROS

When God was made man he had something to suffer, a story
    of a stable, and to weep and be wounded,
Little clogs on great glory, and suddenly he soared
Wide of the Syrians and Romans, and the world that they
    ravaged was an atom in a multitude, surrounded
By the splendor of the dawn's lamps dancing to their Lord.
By the splendor, by the blazing, by the gladness, the brave
    choir of the gods of the morning and the lords of the night,
When he leaned and looked home from the marvelous porches,
And his love like a home-dipping swallow came down from
    the doors of the orient, the mountains of light,
The towers of the dawn that have roses for torches.

ANTICHOROS

No, no. He fell down to his place and has found it, when
    he fainted from the far-stretched limbs of the cross,
And darkness fell home over Golgotha, and God

[201]

Tore in despair the great veil of his temple and regarded not
    what dead men pushed up from the graves
On the hillside ill-hallowed, and grinding brown teeth
On the rottenness of jaws fallen inward ran down on the city
    Jerusalem gibbering and mumbling
Of the earthquake and graves rent and a Roman desolation.

There were five on the hill-slope crying for death or love, and
    one on the height.
Terrible radiations of intense desire streamed up the night.
While the fierce old anger David's father cut through the
    swell and flow
Of the waves of vision deaf and blind. "You coward, I'd
    have let you go.
Couldn't leave the women alone, you dirty coward?" He
    fired, and the breath
Dove-shaped burned at David's mouth to nest in the bosom
    of the splendor of death.
"Father, it doesn't hurt. Love, love, we are mixed in the fire,
    the fire of the world
Ending, heaven beginning, spirits set free, the seas burned,
    the stars hurled.
All the promises have come true. I love you, I love you,
    Lord." He saw
The great vision leaning to kiss his eyes, and cried with de-
    light and awe.

CHOROS

Mountains of Asia you masts of a little bark that floats on a
    firmament of waters,
Himalayas have you seen across the beam-ends of the earth
The master-star of the stars when he brightens at the blos-
    soming of midnight, when he beckons to his daughters,
And they wreathe him with dances when his rays are sent
    forth?

Dark Amazon daughter of the Andes when you flowed full
  flood at the dawn-star when night died on the sea,
When the Andes and the Alps were answering from far,
Broad Volga bride-sister of the Urals, when the Kiolen barked
  answer to Caucasus for the north was made free
Did they speak of that father, of that master, did they point
  at that star?
And an hour before dawn when the night was split open on
  the path of the planets to its height
Did they speak of the guidance of things, and the fury of the
  wings of the speed of the light, and who governs the light?

ANTICHOROS

Lord in the night, in the storm Lord, fear takes hold, hot
  anger bites like a hound
Men's hearts, fearfully rages the storm, loud spirits are
  stirred, lights flicker around,
Lights from the false ghosts' foreheads glitter through night's
  black entrails pricked by the flashes,
Corposant lightnings leap on the crags, live fires on the
  heights that the loud wind lashes.
Lord when our bowels were shrunken, bad passions had
  maimed us, we raised seared eyes from the burning,
No cold Godhead's gaze made answer from heaven but a
  young man's passionate yearning
Stooped to us, beautiful over the storm. More loved is our
  Lord than a lamp in the night,
Sweeter than wild bees' hivings, stronger than storm in the
  mountains, lovelier than light.

There the vision broke, for David's spirit had made it and
  the spirit went out.
Only little noises moved in the night, dim sobbings, walkings
  about.

Only James O'Farrell held fast the purpose that brought him
    to the hill,
Rode across the scattered others, fumbling the horse-hair
    hackamore still.
Reached at dawn the highest pine on the evident peak of the
    hill, and there
Lifted his body from concealment and hanged it up high in
    the white air.
Down the hill they heard the horse run loose, they saw black
    fruit on the tree;
And the river broke its bar, and rushed into the bitter sea.

DIVINELY SUPERFLUOUS BEAUTY

The storm-dances of gulls, the barking game of seals,
Over and under the ocean . . .
Divinely superfluous beauty
Rules the games, presides over destinies, makes trees grow
And hills tower, waves fall.
The incredible beauty of joy
Stars with fire the joining of lips, O let our loves too
Be joined, there is not a maiden
Burns and thirsts for love
More than my blood for you, by the shore of seals while the
    wings
Weave like a web in the air
Divinely superfluous beauty.

THE MAID'S THOUGHT

Why listen, even the water is sobbing for something.
The west wind is dead, the waves
Forget to hate the cliff, in the upland canyons
Whole hillsides burst aglow
With golden broom. Dear how it rained last month,
And every pool was rimmed
With sulphury pollen dust of the wakening pines.
Now tall and slender suddenly
The stalks of purple iris blaze by the brooks,
The penciled ones on the hill;
This deerweed shivers with gold, the white globe-tulips
Blow out their silky bubbles,
But in the next glen bronze-bells nod, the does
Scalded by some hot longing
Can hardly set their pointed hoofs to expect
Love but they crush a flower;
Shells pair on the rock, birds mate, the moths fly double.
O it is time for us now
Mouth kindling mouth to entangle our maiden bodies
To make that burning flower.

FAUNA

I

On the low knoll above the Carmel mouth
A young man was alone he thought, and spoke
A song of how love came from the hot south
In the likeness of a girl, and like a bird
Flew at him from the burning sun and broke
His dream of peace. Dear hills you surely heard,
Pine-crested Santa Lucian hills, although
The old accustomed ocean's tidal flow

Is louder in your sense, and the low wind
Much more melodious than those tones of one
Who dreamed himself alone
And was not so, because a white girl leaned
Listening against a moss-grown bowlder stone.

"Swift love a Marchwind swallow from the south
Came flying, the fleet breath of those burning wings
Blew ash and bitter dust into my mouth
From the heaped hearth, and set my house afire,
I laughed aloud to see the household things
Spoiled by hot violence and insane desire,
And thanked sweet love, merciless love, and gave her
Wine of my grapes to sip and my heart to savor.

"Fauna the sun has kissed your body brown,
The hot south sun, but O I hate the white
Teeth of bold waves that bite
Your shining ankles when you wander down
To dance on the dim shore a moonlit night.

"Because there is one girl's beauty and one girl's mouth
Forbidden me and gainsaid in the eyes of honor,
Swift love a springtime swallow from the south
Came flying and laughing; my numb lips I know
Have strong command to make no trial upon her,
Yet being solitary I may sing low
And thank sweet love, merciless love, and make
Music from lips parched up when my limbs ache

"In the furnace of vain yearning; O April bird
Flown up from the fair south, O fond fleet swallow
Why did you cry me to follow
(You Santa Lucian hills you also heard
That cry) this one prohibited path, a hollow

"Lane leading downward to false caverns dark
Of foreaccurst delight? I will not fare
That way nor task my spirit to tend that spark
Of loveliness that has no word, nor wreathe
One flower but this in the free gold of that hair,
And though for longing I can hardly breathe
I will not speak nor touch, but singing alone
Make useless music shyly and silent moan.

"Fauna the sun has kissed your body brown,
The hot south sun, but O I hate the white
Teeth of those waves that bite
Your dancing ankles when you wander down
Alone under the dunes a moonlit night.

"The gates of her approach are jeweled and golden
Yet for a song I think they would fall down;
Fountains of fortunate waters unbeholden
Jet in the shadowy court on gemlike fronds
Of emerald fern; the sun that burned you brown
Was not my mouth, my mouth is under bonds,
Fauna, and though I sing I may not kiss.
O thank sweet love, merciless love, for this.

"Love that flew up from the south a Marchwind bird,
You Santa Lucian hills moreover saw
The marvel there and the awe,
You Rivers of the South you also heard
The seatides of my sobbing heart withdraw.

"Up in the Carmel Valley are orchards laden
With fragrant apples when rich autumn weather
Hazes the shallowing stream the cattle wade in
And the amber hills and golden shores below,
There by the river ripening all together
The rosy and honey-clustered apples grow;
Fauna that you and I might linger there
When the flushed fruits fall from the glowing air.

"Would God the sun that kissed your body brown
Had been my mouth, Fauna, or mine the white
Teeth of bold waves that bite
Your heedless ankles when you wander down
To dance under the dunes a moonlit night.

"She is not a virgin yet of me she is maiden
Forever; I must lay this chain to heart.
Nor dare we lie in the orchards autumn-laden,
Nor any glade of Santa Lucian leaves
Will shadow our heat of love, we are more apart
Than stone-peaked Grayback whom the high wind grieves
Stands from the autumn-stagnant Carmel's bar,
Or the strong northstar from the Scorpion star.

"Fauna, had fate been cast in finer fashion
The pines of the peninsula would have stirred
To my song, and every bird
By the Rivers of the South echoed my passion,
And the Santa Lucian summit-hills have heard

"The lightest whisper of our love, and bent
Above us for our love's sake to the seas,
While hand in hand under their heights we went
To gather by the Rivers of the South
Cool wreaths of fern and the hoards of perfumed bees
That hive there the right honey for your mouth.
But now because our fates are thus and so,
We must die sundered, we shall never go.

"Fauna, I hate the sun that kissed you brown,
Fauna, I hate the insolent delicate white
Teeth of those waves that bite
Your shining ankles when you wander down
To dance on the dim shore a moonlit night."

II

Then the white girl from her gray bowlder stone:
"What ails you at grief to take delight in it
And make shy music and half silent moan?
When did love care for honor?" And he amazed:
"Love's a wild colt and snaps his teeth on the bit.
The wildest mustang that the mountain grazed
Will tame and take a rider; but I must mind
My honor though love's wilder and though love's blind."

And Nais, with laughter like the drippings of
The little waxen chambers of wild bees:
"O nicely! You are at ease
In your nice fort of honor and know not love,
You men, that is free wind on sweet wild seas.

"Love that forgets in a moment, and remembers
Ten thousand years one pale and sacred face.
That is a golden fisher of pearls and ambers
Out of the monstrous ocean gulfs, but evens

Ghostly remembrance with forgetfulness;
And would scorn honor though in the heaven of heavens
He stared in face of God . . . who should gaze down
Connivingly and frankly, without frown."

"Fauna, the sun has kissed your body brown,
The hot south sun. Dear hills you also heard,
You holier hills, that word.
Sweet Rivers of the South that wander down
Seaward, have you seen love? a wilder bird

"Than the azure keen white-belted kingfisher
Who dives from your dense boughs on dapply trout.
When Fauna passes I go mad for her,
I'd build her a golden house and pave the whole
With rubies from my heart, and all without
Should burn with burnished jewels as a judged soul
In dishonorable hell with fire forever:
And there she'd sleep and I should visit her never.

"Fauna, the sun, the sun that kissed you brown
You must not say that it was not my mouth.
You Rivers of the South
What will you say dear rivers wandering down
Seaward, of my desire and my throat's drouth?"

Then Nais with laughter like the drippings of
Some broken honeycomb of lordless bees:
"My dear you'll find yourself in the house of love
When forty seasons pass! But of this passion
You'll find neither forgetfulness nor ease
Until I set your fates in lovelier fashion
And you in fairer ways and mind more fit
To ride this wild colt whose teeth grind the bit.
[211]

"Was there ever a foal that prayed not to be ridden?
You are the fool to let this foal run free.
Fauna, Fauna . . . is it she
Who loveworthy for loving things forbidden
Was drunk in the deep vineyard over the sea?"

"O," he laughed out, "I saw her there, we saw
The vines trampled under her veering steps,
The vinestocks broken, the wonder there and the awe
When Fauna sang before the gleaners came,
Fettling her choice feet for the chosen grapes,
And dancing under the red sundown flame
Out of the vineyard to the olive hill,
And bidding all the vintage men be still,

"Because the mouth that kissed her body brown
Was not a man's but a great God's the Sun's.
There Nais we snared her once
In the fragrance of the grapes, there she fell down
By the winepress on the heap of hulls and stones."

Then Nais with laughter like crushed honeycomb:
"Would you love me if I'd been drunken there?
Deep in the south your Fauna finds her home,
A gold-ringed wife and childless. But look at me
Unclaimed of man: am I not lovelier,
I northward born not half so brown as she?
I could delight in apples, Fauna had
The purple-hearted grapes to make her glad.

"Up in the Carmel Valley are orchards laden
And glowing with apples in the golden weather,
There let us walk together
Hand clasped in hand, the young man with the maiden,
And love foregoing that Fauna moults no feather."

"With you!" he laughed roughly and ran away
Some forty paces toward the impassioned strand
Where beat on the lank river-bar all day
And break the white-maned racers from the west;
But Nais although he turned not waved her hand;
You Rivers of the South will you attest
The marvel then, the music there and awe?
Dear Santa Lucian hills you also saw.

For while her hand's white forest-flower was shaken,
A Santa Cruz white flagflower, there was heard
Music of flutes that stirred
The mountain, and mazed harps began to awaken
In all the mountain hollows every bird.

And from the sunfall splendor issued a fire
Of hosted voices chanting, and in the south
Strong-throbbing the strung throat of a Greek lyre
Caught up the tune, and northward there was none
To San Francisco harbor's golden mouth
But heard the music gather power and run
On the ocean shore, a triumph of harp and lyre,
Flute, hautboy, fife, and all that feed desire

With sound: sweet Rivers of the South you heard,
Dear Santa Lucian hills you surely saw
The wonder there and the awe
Of spiritual fingers plucking strings and paired
Lovers who drank delight of this new law

And tyranny of struck timbrels turning back
The man's lips to the girl's and love to love.
The sundown splendor died the night was black
And sea-fog blotted the sky's golden swarms,
The waves laughed in the dark and Nais yet strove
On the bare grass in her desire's bare arms
Laughing with brave delights and sobbing low.
Believe or not, the dawn beheld them so.

But soon on dawn a second marvel appeared,
The Mother of Love out of the morning foam
As once of old she had come
Rose: Rivers of the South you also heard
Her tones more rich than new-torn honeycomb.

Dear Santa Lucian hills you also saw
The august and rosy and blameless body arisen
From waters broken, the wonder there and the awe,
The dove-wings and the glory: but what she said
I may not now repeat, but as from prison
It loosed that lover, then his doubts were dead
And having learned of Nais the way to woo
He'll flower in time and fling at Fauna too.

Fauna, the sun to burn her body brown
That is his mouth, nor must he hate the white
Teeth of bold waves that bite
Her dancing ankles if she wander down
Love-drunken near the dunes a moonlit night.

III

"When I crossed the seaward valley, by a sudden lightening
    of the moon
I saw very love
There in Fauna incarnate, and the wind uttered a cry, the
    waves a tune,
Wild swans cried above.
I saw love incarnate, all the beauty and all the cruelty and
    all the splendor.
Where her sandals trod
On the creek-bed stones were gold and fire embracing but
    between her tender
Breasts were Christ and God.
At her heels the leaping she-wolf that she feeds and keeps
    for her companion

Followed, tawny and fierce.
When the noise of barking seals on Soberanes rocks came up
the canyon
Her wild friend pricked ears.
'Fauna, lately I learned of little Nais the way to love, O
Fauna, love me!'
So I cried, but laughter,
Vanishing laughter answered, she was gone, I heard the wild
swans crying above me
And the wolf's growl after.
Blindly I sought her through the valley and in the mountains
for the moon had vanished
And her feet were soundless.
Blindly I seek and wander through the beautiful peninsula
like a banished
Spirit in waste and boundless
Demon-visited deserts, while desire in my dry throat cries
Dearest where
Do your wild feet wander?
By what streamside in what forest flows the drunken fra-
grance of your hair
For dull winds to squander?
Though I've asked the southwind and have questioned the
eastwind and the north concerning her
And besought the sea,
None responds, yet surely at some ford or mountainhead she
falters, turning her
Footsteps home to me.
Woodpeckers that thrid the wildwood branches, bluejays with
black helmet-crests,
Vultures of the sun,
Underforest wildflowers have you felt her feet, birds have
you seen her breasts
Flash or bright feet run?
Tell her that I've slashed the face of honor for desire to kiss
her feet,
But to embrace her bodily

I being thoroughly mad would give myself to torture, or to
    taste her sweet
Lie in the windrows bloodily,
Downed by despicable death in the place where the equal-
    minded warmen meet,
And the Mother of Love smiles moodily."

IV

"Ah drunken Fauna I knew I'd find you here
In the deep vineyard tasting sunburnt grapes
And hidden among the sixfoot vines." "My dear
You knew me wisely but you've waited long.
The hour flashes and goes by, the girl escapes
Who timely tempted might have done some wrong
To honor, a kiss or so." "A kiss or two!"
"When little Nais was teaching you to woo,

"(A shameless one, that wanton) did you swear
Because the sun had kissed my body brown
Your mouth must do it?" "I'll own,
Witch, that you've wound me up in your bright hair."
"When you dared fling at her the bird was flown."

"A golden-feathered bird but wild and wild."
"Too shy for stupid fowlers to pursue."
"Wine-hearted Fauna, honey-throated child
What would the farmer say if he should come
And find us in his fragrant vineyard, you
Nibbling the fruit and me with finger and thumb
Squirting the juice into your breast?" "He'd say
'Boys, chase the man with sticks, the girl may stay.'"

"Fauna, let's cut the ripest clusters, these
Sun-colored as your round throat's loveliness,
And hide them in your dress
To share them yonder under the olive trees
Or the noon coolness of the cypresses."

"Those clusters were too ripe, a purple dew
Ran down between my breasts and stained the cloth.
Take out your hand. I will not walk with you
Anywhere under trees, I would not dare."
"My hand is trembling like a foolish moth
That touched flame." "Yet the grapes lie sweetly there
Between my breasts." "Come, Fauna, to the pool
Below the thicket liveoak trees, with cool

"Clear water underneath the shadowy hill
We'll wash those winestains from the well-dyed cloth."
"Dear, first will you take oath
To touch only my hands (or if you will
My lips perhaps) not more?" "I will kiss both

"Your hands and lips, come Fauna." Hand in hand
They passed through the hot vines and up the hill
Out of the sun to where clear waters stand
In a stone basin under braided leaves.
There they could smell the vineyard fragrance still,
But saw what fairy patterns the sun weaves
On standing water when his rays are shed
Through weft of tangled foliage overhead.

"Dear love your mouth is hot and you kiss more
Than lips or hands." "Sweet but no further down
Than the round throat or brown
Shoulders." "But you took oath." "I never swore."
"Ah the ground's soaking here, you'll soil my gown."

"It was already stained with shameless wine,
We'll wash it soon." "Traitor, you've torn it, too."
"O Fauna, Fauna, mine and mine and mine
Forever." "Listen, someone's coming!" "No,
The oakleaves murmur." "Why will you undo
The girdle as well? Sweet dearest let me go,
You have nearly made me naked." "Love, love, love!"
"O kiss me now! Kill me, it is not enough,

[217]

"Why should I live?" "Ah, Fauna." So they whispered
Together in the high noon solemn and hushed.
The pulpy grapes were crushed
That lay between her breast; a gentle lisp heard
From far of falling water charmed the flushed

Young wealth of amorous limbs trembling together;
No other sound through all the oaken grove
Moved, but their breathing. High in the bright blue weather
White awful wings kept watch lest man come near;
And other angel-ministers of love
Strode with drawn blades of metal blazing-clear
Silent through the oaks and cypresses, to guard
The sacred sleep that should come afterward.

"Fauna, the sun to kiss your body brown,
Feel it, my mouth. Fauna but let me bite
Those secret spots and white
The sun's lips never fondled." "All's your own,
You have nothing yet, all, all, O dear delight."

As harp-music and flutes made rich for Nais
Her northward joy, noon silence more august
And timeless wreaths made this; *maile leis*
From fern forests above Hawaiian strands
By no keel ferried but by the instant thrust
Of divine wings were borne: no woman's hands
Wove, odorous of the utmost ocean-west,
Those sacred wreaths; and from the sad red east

Cornflowers of Picardy with man's blood fed,
Pansies burnt brown with orphan tears, were brought,
And hyacinths too well wrought
With letters of the weary Alas then spread
World over beyond all wings of weeping thought.

Wide-flaunting poppies from the purpled fields
Between the Marne and Meuse; and with them came
Lake Como windflowers, and the honeyed yields
Of Tuscan hillsides and Calabrian dales;
And crocuses of vari-colored flame
From Africa; but the Siculian vales
Sent all their fairest spring, to flower again
Neither on Ætna slopes nor Enna plain.

And out of battle-islanded Switzerland,
Obeying the Mother alpine roses flew
And hard white stars that grew
Higher up than ever a chamois-hunter's hand
Reached, on the crag-lip in the giddy blue

Above the crevassed glacier. And here gathered
Arab frankincense buds and Syrian myrrh,
With mazy seaflowers that the seafoam fathered
In warm live waters south the Hydaspian gulf,
They fell like snowflakes from the flaming air,
And frightened by the wonder Fauna's wolf
That still had watched, ran off. From the upper Nile
Came lotoses, and laurels from Lesbos isle.

Great lilies from large Asia congregated
Amazed the tolerant vintage-month with massed
Mounds of May sweet; the vast
Sky-heads of the earth-out-of-mind Himalaya mated
Their snow-buds with starved bloom Siberia cast.

And soon came homelier and more kindly blossoms,
Orchids from under the Araucanian Andes
Were forced into the beauty of Fauna's bosoms,
Through her good sleep, where the crushed grapes had lain,
But maidenly in the opening of her hand is
A white globe-tulip fainting without stain,
Fed from peninsular forests of Monterey,
And at her feet white flagflowers fainted away,

The Santa Cruz wood-irises; and brown
As her sunned body and excellent as her mouth
Was mingled a new growth,
Bronze-bells of redwood darknesses that drown
The Santa Lucian Rivers of the South.

While hermit yuccas from La Cumbre wasted
Flaked petal-wealth and faint white fragrance there,
Young sand-verbena from south shores was tasted
Intense among the perfumes, native poppies
Paled in the splendor of the spun-gold hair,
Wild yellow violets of the liveoak coppice
Flowered up through all, strange-shapen and blood-red
Were phallic snowplants on the perfumed bed

Strown for a laughing symbol; from the south
They also, from the firforest that grows
About Bear Lake or close
Under cold Grayback; and with that uncouth
Male flower mated the moist and female rose.

And crested serpents from the vineyard creeping,
And cold striped snakes out of the cistern came,
And pierced the flowers and found the lovers sleeping
In sacred joy; with jewel-like eyes they gazed,
And fondled them with forky tongues aflame,
And drunk with blended fragrances upraised
Each one his dainty hard and carven head
To hiss good blessings on the bridal bed.

So from new moon until the next moon quickened
Innumerably incorruptible
The flowers remained, nor fell
A single petal nor one perfume sickened.
Fair lovers in the favored bed farewell.

THE SONGS OF THE DEAD MEN TO THE
THREE DANCERS

I. TO DESIRE

(Here a dancer enters and dances.

Who is she that is fragrant and desirable,
Clothed but enough to wake wantonness,
And proud of her polished lithe body and her narrowing of
kohl-darkened eyelids with arrows between them?
Ah, ah, ah! Goddess of the world,
Young serpent in the veins of the rock,
In the mountain of jewels a young serpent, in the veins of
a man a sweet viper all emerald: ah Goddess
Are we proof to the hilt, are you pleased with us
When the splendor of your undulant insolence
Pricks the dark entrails of death, his foregathered grow hot
for you, the skeleton stands up to be amorous?
Ah, ah, ah! Goddess of the flesh
Will you think it a gift lacking grace
That the gates of the grave have been battered before you,
the iron doors to us dead in the deepest abysm?
For who has gone down to the dead or has touched them?
Did Jesus of Nazareth when he lay in deep hell
For three days and since lived as they say and has failed us?
No man nor no woman has gone down to us dead
Living until now, but the proof is here now, ah beautiful
torture us again and again.
We are fleshless, we tremble to your flesh,
Dear Goddess to taste of the dew
On your arms when you dance or to lip at the glitter of your
burnished thighs or the breast of your barrenness.

In the book of your triumphs with no term
Inscribe a more wonderful deed,
That you quickened the dead, that you lifted the flesh of the
    fleshless, ah Goddess, ah! dancing, us dead men.

> (The dancer goes out.

II. TO DEATH

> (A second dancer enters and dances.

Was it lovely to lie among violets ablossom in the valleys of
    love on the breast of the south?
It was lovely but lovelier now
To behold the calm head of the dancer we dreaded, his curls
    are as tendrils of the vineyard, O Death
Sweet and more sweet is your dancing.
Like the swoon of fulfilment of love in some lonelier vale
    among flowers is the languor that flushes us,
O why did we fear him, for Death
Is a beautiful youth and his eyes are sleepy, the lids droop
    heavily with wine when he wakens,
And his breast is more smooth than a dove's.
Fair Garda, gay water with olives engarlanded, lake of blue
    laughter in a bay of the Alps
It is better for our spirits to be here
In the desolate hollows of darkness beholding the beauty of
    our dancer than at rest on your hills
Of anemones and jonquils immingled.
And gay from the glacier womb, boy-throated for gladness
    to shout where the snow-crags throng
Ran foaming the rivulet Rhone,
When the mountains were sprung for his passage, the ridges
    of granite were splintered; and lovely the lake was
Under the vineyards of Vaud,
And at evening empurpling the peaks of the Chablais were
    painted on the sleep and deep shadow of its waters
When the sundown was flame on la Dole.

But the best of the course is the last broad slumber, O river
    of France to forget and go down
Slow-gliding and sultrily stagnant
Past Arles to the Gulf of the Lion and that azure and beauti-
    ful grave in the waves of the south
That are warmest and best . . . and an end . . .
                    (The dancer has gone out.

III. TO VICTORY

            (A third dancer enters and dances.
Use us again, you in the world only of goddesses worshipful
    now or adored,
Helmeted victory!
How did we bow, even in dream, visions betraying us, unto
    some other and base
Power when your splendor there
Struck on the gates? Use us again, awfully beautiful. Blood
    will reblossom from death
Burning to minister
All its revived fire at your feet, only to merit an eye-glance,
    or flash of your hand's
Gauntleted majesty.
Pounding of guns clear you a path, trample the ports of
    decision and triumph on the slain.
Men when they fall in it
Gayly they die, scattering for flowers rosy and white at your
    feet the red blood and pale brains
Carpeting battlefields.
Towering in steel, terribly armed, which of the daughters of
    heaven is so hotly desired?
None has embraced you yet,
All of us burn, beautifully mad, frantic with lust of your
    beauty and with thirst of your mouth's
Terrible maidenhood;
Holy and white, under the steel, hide the sweet limbs of our
    longing desire in a deep

[223]

Sacred virginity.
Emperors and lords gave her in vain cities of gold and whole
   nations of blood, for she took
Gifts, but rejected them.
Neither a king's bribe nor a bold armorer's hammer prevails
   to unrivet the steel
Belt of her maidenhood,
Yet shall our prayer surely be heard. Goddess of glory revoke
   our exemption of death,
Twice let us die for you.
Use us again, though but an hour: surely the prayer is as
   humble as the gift would be great,
Helmeted Victory.

                              (The dancer goes out.

TO HIS FATHER

Christ was your lord and captain all your life,
He fails the world but you he did not fail,
He led you through all forms of grief and strife
Intact, a man full-armed, he let prevail
Nor outward malice nor the worse-fanged snake
That coils in one's own brain against your calm,
That great rich jewel well guarded for his sake
With coronal age and death like quieting balm.
I Father having followed other guides
And oftener to my hurt no leader at all,
Through years nailed up like dripping panther hides
For trophies on a savage temple wall
Hardly anticipate that reverend stage
Of life, the snow-wreathed honor of extreme age.

THE TRUCE AND THE PEACE
(November, 1918)

1

Peace now for every fury has had her day,
Their natural make is moribund, they cease,
They carry the inward seeds of quick decay,
Build breakwaters for storm but build on peace.
The mountains' peace answers the peace of the stars,
Our petulances are cracked against their term.
God built our peace and plastered it with wars,
Those frescoes fade, flake off, peace remains firm.
In the beginning before light began
We lay or fluttered blind in burdened wombs,
And like that first so is the last of man,
When under death for husband the amorous tombs
Are covered and conceive; nine months go by
No midwife called, nine years no baby's cry.

2

Peace now, though purgatory fires were hot
They always had a heart something like ice
That coldly peered and wondered, suffering not
Nor pleased in any park, nor paradise
Of slightly swelling breasts and beautiful arms
And throat engorged with very carnal blood.
It coldly peered and wondered, "Strong God your charms
Are glorious, I remember solitude.
Before youth towered we knew a time of truth
To have eyes was nearly rapture." Peace now, for war
Will find the cave that childhood found and youth.

Ten million lives are stolen and not one star
Dulled; wars die out, life will die out, death cease,
Beauty lives always and the beauty of peace.

8

Peace to the world in time or in a year,
In the inner world I have touched the instant peace.
Man's soul's a flawless crystal coldly clear,
A cool white mansion that he yields in lease
To tenant dreams and tyrants from the brain
And riotous burnings of the lovelier flesh.
We pour strange wines and purples all in vain.
The crystal remains pure, the mansion flesh.
All the Asian bacchanals and those from Thrace
Lived there and left no wine-mark on the walls.
What were they doing in that more sacred place
All the Asian and the Thracian bacchanals?
Peace to the world to-morrow or in a year,
Peace in that mansion white, that crystal clear.

4

Peace now poor earth. They fought for freedom's sake,
She was starving in a corner while they fought.
They knew not whom they stabbed by Onega Lake,
Whom lashed from Archangel, whom loved, whom sought.
How can she die, she is the blood unborn,
The energy in earth's arteries beating red,
The world will flame with her in some great morn,
The whole great world flame with her, and we be dead.
Here in the west it grows by dim degrees,
In the east flashed and will flame terror and light.
Peace now poor earth, peace to that holier peace
Deep in the soul held secret from all sight.
That crystal, the pure home, the holier peace,
Fires flaw not, scars the cruelest cannot crease.

South of the Big Sur River up the hill
Three graves are marked thick weeds and grasses heap,
Under the forest there I have stood still
Hours, thinking it the sweetest place to sleep . . .
Strewing all-sufficient death with compliments
Sincere and unrequired, coveting peace . . .
Boards at the head not stones, the text's rude paints
Mossed, rain-rubbed . . . wasting hours of scanty lease
To admire their peace made perfect. From that height
But for the trees the whole valley might be seen,
But for the heavy dirt, the eye-pits no light
Enters, the heavy dirt, the grass growing green
Over the dirt, the molelike secretness,
The immense withdrawal, the dirt, the quiet, the peace.

6

Women cried that morning, bells rocked with mirth,
We all were glad a long while afterward,
But still in dreary places of the earth
A hundred hardly fed shall labor hard
To clothe one belly and stuff it with soft meat,
Blood paid for peace but still those poor shall buy it,
This sweat of slaves is no good wine but yet
Sometimes it climbs to the brain. Be happy and quiet,
Be happy and live, be quiet or God might wake.
He sleeps in the mountain that is heart of man's heart,
He also in promontory fists, and make
Of stubborn-muscled limbs, he will not start
For a little thing . . . his great hands grope, unclose,
Feel out for the main pillars . . . pull down the house . . .

7

After all, after all we endured, who has grown wise?
We take our mortal momentary hour

With too much gesture, the derisive skies
Twinkle against our wrongs, our rights, our power.
Look up the night, starlight's a steadying draught
For nerves at angry tension. They have all meant well,
Our enemies and the knaves at whom we've laughed,
The liars, the clowns in office, the kings in hell,
They have all meant well in the main . . . some of them
    tried
The mountain road of tolerance . . . They have made war,
Conspired, oppressed, robbed, murdered, lied and lied,
Meant well, played the loud fool . . . and star by star
Winter Orion pursues the Pleiades
In pale and huge parade, silence and peace.

8

That ice within the soul, the admonisher
Of madness when we're wildest, the unwinking eye
That measures all things with indifferent stare,
Choosing far stars to check near objects by,
That quiet lake inside and underneath,
Strong, undisturbed by any angel of strife,
Being so tranquil seems the presence of death,
Being so central seems the essence of life.
Is it perhaps that death and life make truce
In neutral zone while their old feud beyond
Fires the towered cities? Surely for a strange use
He sphered that eye of flawless diamond.
It does not serve him but with line and rod
Measures him, how indeed should God serve God?

9

It does not worship him, it will not serve.
And death and life within that Eye combine,
Within that only untorturable nerve
Of those that make a man, within that shrine

Which there is nothing ever can profane,
Where life and death are sister and brother and lovers,
The golden voice of Christ were heard in vain,
The holy spirit of God visibly hovers.
Small-breasted girls, lithe women heavy-haired,
Loves that once grew into our nerves and veins,
Yours Freedom was desire that deeper dared
To the citadel where mastery remains,
Yours to the spirit . . . discount the penny that is
Ungivable, this Eye, this God, this Peace.

10

All in a simple innocence I strove
To give myself away to any power,
Wasting on women's bodies wealth of love,
Worshipping every sunrise mountain tower;
Some failure mocked me still denying perfection,
Parts of me might be spended not the whole,
I sought of wine surrender and self-correction,
I failed, I could not give away my soul.
Again seeking to give myself I sought
Outward in vain through all things, out through God,
And tried all heights, all gulfs, all dreams, all thought.
I found this wisdom on the wonderful road,
The essential Me cannot be given away,
The single Eye, God cased in blood-shot clay.

11

Peace to the world in time or in a year,
But always all our lives this peace was ours.
Peace is not hard to have, it lies more near
Than breathing to the breast. When brigand powers
Of anger or pain or the sick dream of sin
Break our soul's house outside the ruins we weep.

We look through the breached wall, why there within
All the red while our peace was lying asleep.
Smiling in dreams while the broad knives drank blood,
The robbers triumphed, the roof burned overhead,
The eternal living and untroubled God
Lying asleep upon a lily bed.
Men screamed, the bugles screamed, walls broke in the air,
We never knew till then that He was there.

NATURAL MUSIC

The old voice of the ocean, the bird-chatter of little rivers,
(Winter has given them gold for silver
To stain their water and bladed green for brown to line their
    banks)
From different throats intone one language.
So I believe if we were strong enough to listen without
Divisions of desire and terror
To the storm of the sick nations, the rage of the hunger-
    smitten cities,
Those voices also would be found
Clean as a child's; or like some girl's breathing who dances
    alone
By the ocean-shore, dreaming of lovers.

POINT JOE

Point Joe has teeth and has torn ships; it has fierce and
    solitary beauty;
Walk there all day you shall see nothing that will not make
    part of a poem.

I saw the spars and planks of shipwreck on the rocks, and
    beyond the desolate
Sea-meadows rose the warped wind-bitten van of the pines,
    a fog-bank vaulted

Forest and all, the flat sea-meadows at that time of year
    were plated
Golden with the low flower called footsteps of the spring,
    millions of flowerets,

Whose light suffused upward into the fog flooded its vault,
    we wandered
Through a weird country where the light beat up from earth-
    ward, and was golden.

One other moved there, an old Chinaman gathering seaweed
    from the sea-rocks,
He brought it in his basket and spread it flat to dry on the
    edge of the meadow.

Permanent things are what is needful in a poem, things
    temporally
Of great dimension, things continually renewed or always
    present.

Grass that is made each year equals the mountains in her
   past and future;
Fashionable and momentary things we need not see nor
   speak of.

Man gleaning food between the solemn presences of land and
   ocean,
On shores where better men have shipwrecked, under fog
   and among flowers,

Equals the mountains in his past and future; that glow
   from the earth was only
A trick of nature's, one must forgive nature a thousand
   graceful subtleties.

POINT PINOS AND POINT LOBOS

I

A lighthouse and a graveyard and gaunt pines
Not old, no tree lives long here, where the northwind
Has forgot mercy. All night the light blinks north,
The Santa Cruz mountain redwoods hate its flashing,
The night of the huge western water takes it,
The long rays drown a little off shore, hopelessly
Attempting distance, hardly entering the ocean.
The lighthouse, and the gaunt boughs of the pines,
The carved gray stones, and the people of the graves.

They came following the sun, here even the sun is bitter,
A scant gray heartless light down wind, glitter and sorrow,
The northwind fog much kindlier. When shall these dead
    arise,
What day stand up from the earth among the broken pines?
A God rearisen will raise them up, this walking shadow?
Which tortured trunk will you choose, Lord, to be hewn to a
    cross?
I am not among the mockers Master, I am one of your
    lovers,
Ah weariest spirit in all the world, we all have rest
Being dead but you still strive, nearly two thousand years
You have wrestled for us against God, were you not con-
    quered
At the first close, when the long horrible nails went home
Between the slender bones of the hands and feet, you fright-
    fully

Heightened above man's stature saw the hateful crowd
Shift and sicken below, the sunburnt legionaries
Draw back out of the blood-drops . . . Far off the city
Slid on its hill, the eyes fainting. The earth was shaken
And the sun hid, you were not quieted. Men may never
Have seen you as they said in the inner room of the house,
Nor met you on the dusty suburb road toward Emmaus,
But nine years back you stood in the Alps and wept for
    Europe,
To-day pale ghost you walk among the tortured pines
Between the graves here and the sea.

                    Ah but look seaward,
For here where the land's charm dies love's chain falls loose,
    and the freedom of the eyes and the fervor of the spirit
Sea-hawks wander the huge gray water, alone in a nihilist
    simplicity, cleaner than the primal
Wings of the brooding of the dove on the waste of the waters
    beginning, perplexed with creation; but ours
Turned from creation, returned from the beauty of things to
    the beauty of nothing, to a nihilist simplicity,
Content with two elements, the wave and the cloud, and if
    one were not there then the other were lovelier to turn to,
And if neither . . . O shining of night, O eloquence of si-
    lence, the mother of the stars, the beauty beyond beauty,
The sea that the stars and the sea and the mountain bones
    of the earth and men's souls are the foam on, the opening
Of the womb of that ocean.

            You have known this, you have known peace, and
    forsaken
Peace for pity, you have known the beauty beyond beauty
And the other shore of God. You will never again know
    them,
Except he slay you, the spirit at last, as more than once
The body, and root out love. Is it for this you wander

Tempting him through the thickets of the wolvish world?
O a last time in the last wrench of man made godlike
Shall God not rise, bitterly, the power behind power, the last
    star
That the stars hide, rise and reveal himself in anger—
Christ, in that moment when the hard loins of your ancient
Love and unconquerable will crack to lift up humanity
The last step heavenward—rise and slay, and you and our
    children
Suddenly stumble on peace? The oceans we shall have tamed
    then
Will dream between old rocks having no master, the earth
Forget corn, dreaming her own precious weeds and free
Forests, from the rivers upward; our tributary planets
Tamed like the earth, the morning star and the many-mooned
Three-belted giant, and those red sands of Mars between
    them,
Rust off the metal links of human conquest, the engines
Rust in the fields, and under that old sun's red waning
Nothing forever remember us.

            And you at peace then
Not walk by a lighthouse on a wild north foreland
Choosing which trunk of the poor wind-warped pines
Will hew to a cross, and your eye's envy searching
The happiness of these bleak burials. Unhappy brother
That high imagination mating mine
Has gazed deeper than graves: is it unendurable
To know that the huge season and wheel of things
Turns on itself forever, the new stars pass
And the old return and find out their old places,
And these gray dead infallibly shall arise
In the very flesh . . . But first the camel bells
Tinkle into Bethlehem, the men from the east
Gift you sweet-bedded between Mary's breasts,
And no one in the world has thought of Golgotha.

II

Gray granite ridges over swinging pits of sea, pink stone-
crop spangles

Stick in the stone, the stiff plates of the cypress-boughs divide
the sea's breath,

Hard green cutting soft gray . . . I know the uplands

And windy pastures where the great globes of the oaks are
like green planets

Each in his place; I know the scents and resonances of deso-
late hills,

The wide-winged shadows of the vultures wandering across
them; and I have visited

Deserts and many-colored rocks . . . mountains I know

From the Dent d'Oche in Savoy and that peak of the south
past Saint Gingolphe

To Grayback and Tahoma . . . as for sea-borderers

The caverned Norman cliffs north of the Seine's mouth, the
Breton sea-heads, the Cornish

Horns of their west had known me as a child before I knew
Point Dume or Pinos

Or Sur, the sea-light in his forehead: also I heard my masters

Speak of Pelorum head and the Attic rocks of Sunium, or
that Nymphæan

Promontory under the holy mountain Athos, a warren of
monks

Walls in with prayer-cells of old stone, perpetual incense
and religion

Smoke from it up to him who is greater than they guess,
through what huge emptiness

And chasms above the stars seeking out one who is here
already, and neither

Ahunting nor asleep nor in love; and Actium and the Acro-
ceraunian

And Chersonese abutments of Greek ridges on the tideless
wave

They named, my spirit has visited . . . there is no place

Taken like this out of deep Asia for a marriage-token, this
planted
Asiaward over the west water. Our race nor the great springs
we draw from,
Not any race of Europe, nor the Syrian blood from south
of Lebanon
Our fathers drank and mixed with ours, has known this
place nor its like nor suffered
The air of its religion. The elder shapes and shows in ex-
treme Asia,
Like remote mountains over immeasurable water, half seen,
thought clouds,
Of God in the huge world from the Altai eagle-peaks and
Mongol pastures
To the home of snow no wing inhabits, temples of height
on earth, Gosainthan
And Gaurisankar north of Ganges, Nanda Devi a mast of
the ship
We voyage upon among the stars; and the earth-sprung
multitudes of India,
Where human bodies grow like weeds out of the earth, and
life is nothing,
There is so much life, and like the people the divinities of
the people
Swarm, and the vulgar worship; thence far east to the islands
of this ocean
Our sun is buried in, theirs born of, to the noble slope of
the lone peak
Over Suruga Bay, and the headlands of Hai-nan: God with-
out name,
God without form, the Lord of Asia, is here as there.

Serenely smiling
Face of the godlike man made God, who tore the web of
human passions
As a yellow lion the antelope-hunter's net, and freeing him-
self made free

[289]

All who could follow, the tissue of new births and deaths
    dissolved away from him,
He reunited with the passionless light sky, not again to
    suffer
The shame of the low female gate, freed, never to be born
    again,
Whom Maha Maya bore in the river garden, the Himalayan
    barrier northward
Bounding the world: is it freedom, smile of the Buddha,
    surely freedom? For someone
Whispered into my ear when I was very young, some serpent
    whispered
That what has gone returns; what has been, is; what will
    be, was; the future
Is a farther past; our times he said fractions of arcs of the
    great circle;
And the wheel turns, nothing shall stop it nor destroy it,
    we are bound on the wheel,
We and the stars and seas, the mountains and the Buddha.
    Weary tidings
To cross the weary, bitter to bitter men: life's conqueror
    will not fear
Life; and to meditate again under the sacred tree, and again
Vanquish desire will be no evil.

            The evening opens
Enormous wings out of the west, the sad red splendid light
    beats upward
These granite gorges, the wind-battered cypress trees blacken
    above them,
The divine image of my dream smiles his immortal peace,
    commanding
This old sea-garden, crumble of granite and old buttressed
    cypress trunks,
And the burnt place where that wild girl whose soul was
    fire died with her house.

III

I have spoken on sea-forelands with the lords of life, the
    men wisdom made Gods had nothing
So wise to tell me nor so sweet as the alternation of white
    sunlight and brown night,
The beautiful succession of the breeding springs, the enor-
    mous rhythm of the stars' deaths
And fierce renewals: O why were you rebellious, teachers
    of men, against the instinctive God,
One striving to overthrow his ordinances through love and
    the other crafty-eyed to escape them
Through patient wisdom: though you are wiser than all men
    you are foolisher than the running grass,
That fades in season and springs up in season, praising
    whom you blame.

          For the essence and the end
Of his labor is beauty, for goodness and evil are two things
    and still variant, but the quality of life as of death and
    of light
As of darkness is one, one beauty, the rhythm of that Wheel,
    and who can behold it is happy and will praise it to the
    people.

NOT OUR GOOD LUCK

Not our good luck nor the instant peak and fulfilment of
    time gives us to see
The beauty of things, nothing can bridle it.
God who walks lightning-naked on the Pacific has never
    been hidden from any
Puddle or hillock of the earth behind us.
Between the mean mud tenements and huddle of the filth of
    Babylon the river Euphrates;
And over the tiled brick temple buttresses
And the folly of a garden on arches, the ancienter simple and
    silent tribe of the stars
Filed, and for all her gods and the priests' mouths
God also moved on the city; or a certain young tribesman
    come down from the mountains of the north
Espied him in the eyes of a temple harlot;
Whom presently, as then, when the priests have choked him
    with perfume some prophet like a desert camel
Shall talk with in the ridges above the rock-tombs.

Dark ships drawing in from the sundown and the islands
    of the south, great waves with gray vapor in your hollows
And whitening of high heads coming home from the west,
From Formosa or the skerries of Siberia and the sight of
    the eyes that have widened for the sky-peaks of Asia:
That he touched you is no wonder, that you slid from his
    hand
Is an old known tale to our foreland cypresses, no news
    to the Lobos granite, no marvel
To Point Pinos Light and the beacon at Point Sur.

But here is the marvel, he is nowhere not present, his beauty,
    it is burning in the midland villages
And tortures men's eyes in the alleys of cities.

Far-flown ones, you children of the hawk's dream future
    when you lean from a crag of the last planet on the
    ocean
Of the far stars, remember we also have known beauty.

THE CYCLE

The clapping blackness of the wings of pointed cormorants,
    the great indolent planes
Of autumn pelicans nine or a dozen strung shorelong,
But chiefly the gulls, the cloud-caligraphers of windy spirals
    before a storm,
Cruise north and south over the sea-rocks and over
That bluish enormous opal; very lately these alone, these
    and the clouds
And westering lights of heaven, crossed it; but then
A hull with standing canvas crept about Point Lobos . . .
    now all day long the steamers
Smudge the opal's rim; often a seaplane troubles
The sea-wind with its throbbing heart. These will increase,
    the others diminish; and later
These will diminish; our Pacific have pastured
The Mediterranean torch and passed it west across the
    fountains of the morning;
And the following desolation that feeds on Crete
Feed here; the clapping blackness of the wings of pointed
    cormorants, the great sails
Of autumn pelicans, the gray sea-going gulls,
Alone will streak the enormous opal, the earth have peace
    like the broad water, our blood's
Unrest have doubled to Asia and be peopling
Europe again, or dropping colonies at the morning star:
    what moody traveler
Wanders back here, watches the sea-fowl circle
The old sea-granite and cemented granite with one regard,
    and greets my ghost,
One temper with the granite, bulking about here?

SALMON-FISHING

The days shorten, the south blows wide for showers now,
The south wind shouts to the rivers,
The rivers open their mouths and the salt salmon
Race up into the freshet.
In Christmas month against the smoulder and menace
Of a long angry sundown,
Red ash of the dark solstice, you see the anglers,
Pitiful, cruel, primeval,
Like the priests of the people that built Stonehenge,
Dark silent forms, performing
Remote solemnities in the red shallows
Of the river's mouth at the year's turn,
Drawing landward their live bullion, the bloody mouths
And scales full of the sunset
Twitch on the rocks, no more to wander at will
The wild Pacific pasture nor wanton and spawning
Race up into fresh water.

TO THE HOUSE

I am heaping the bones of the old mother
To build us a hold against the host of the air;
Granite the blood-heat of her youth
Held molten in hot darkness against the heart
Hardened to temper under the feet
Of the ocean cavalry that are maned with snow
And march from the remotest west.
This is the primitive rock, here in the wet
Quarry under the shadow of waves
Whose hollows mouthed the dawn; little house each stone
Baptized from that abysmal font
The sea and the secret earth gave bonds to affirm you.

TO THE ROCK THAT WILL BE A CORNERSTONE
OF THE HOUSE

Old garden of grayish and ochre lichen,
How long a time since the brown people who have vanished
   from here
Built fires beside you and nestled by you
Out of the ranging sea-wind?   A hundred years, two hun-
   dred,
You have been dissevered from humanity
And only known the stubble squirrels and the headland rab-
   bits,
Or the long-fetlocked plowhorses
Breaking the hilltop in December, sea-gulls following,
Screaming in the black furrow; no one
Touched you with love, the gray hawk and the red hawk
   touched you
Where now my hand lies. So I have brought you
Wine and white milk and honey for the hundred years of
   famine
And the hundred cold ages of sea-wind.

I did not dream the taste of wine could bind with granite,
Nor honey and milk please you; but sweetly
They mingle down the storm-worn cracks among the mosses,
Interpenetrating the silent
Wind-prints of ancient weathers long at peace, and the older
Scars of primal fire, and the stone
Endurance that is waiting millions of years to carry

A corner of the house, this also destined.
Lend me the stone strength of the past and I will lend you
The wings of the future, for I have them.
How dear you will be to me when I too grow old, old
    comrade.

TO THE STONE-CUTTERS

Stone-cutters fighting time with marble, you foredefeated
Challengers of oblivion
Eat cynical earnings, knowing rock splits, records fall down,
The square-limbed Roman letters
Scale in the thaws, wear in the rain. The poet as well
Builds his monument mockingly;
For man will be blotted out, the blithe earth die, the brave
    sun
Die blind, his heart blackening:
Yet stones have stood for a thousand years, and pained
    thoughts found
The honey peace in old poems.

SUICIDE'S STONE

Peace is the heir of dead desire,
Whether abundance killed the cormorant
In a happy hour, or sleep or death
Drowned him deep in dreamy waters,
Peace is the ashes of that fire,
The heir of that king, the inn of that journey.

This last and best and goal: we dead
Hold it so tight you are envious of us
And fear under sunk lids contempt.
Death-day greetings are the sweetest.
Let trumpets roar when a man dies
And rockets fly up, he has found his fortune.

Yet hungering long and pitiably
That way, you shall not reach a finger
To pluck it unripe and before dark
Creep to cover: life broke ten whipstocks
Over my back, broke faith, stole hope,
Before I denounced the covenant of courage.

WISE MEN IN THEIR BAD HOURS

Wise men in their bad hours have envied
The little people making merry like grasshoppers
In spots of sunlight, hardly thinking
Backward but never forward, and if they somehow
Take hold upon the future they do it
Half asleep, with the tools of generation
Foolishly reduplicating
Folly in thirty-year periods; they eat and laugh too,
Groan against labors, wars and partings,
Dance, talk, dress and undress; wise men have pretended
The summer insects enviable;
One must indulge the wise in moments of mockery.
Strength and desire possess the future,
The breed of the grasshopper shrills, "What does the future
Matter, we shall be dead?"   Ah, grasshoppers,
Death's a fierce meadowlark: but to die having made
Something more equal to the centuries
Than muscle and bone, is mostly to shed weakness.
The mountains are dead stone, the people
Admire or hate their stature, their insolent quietness,
The mountains are not softened nor troubled
And a few dead men's thoughts have the same temper.

CONTINENT'S END

At the equinox when the earth was veiled in a late rain,
  wreathed with wet poppies, waiting spring,
The ocean swelled for a far storm and beat its boundary,
  the ground-swell shook the beds of granite.

I gazing at the boundaries of granite and spray, the estab-
  lished sea-marks, felt behind me
Mountain and plain, the immense breadth of the continent,
  before me the mass and doubled stretch of water.

I said: You yoke the Aleutian seal-rocks with the lava and
  coral sowings that flower the south,
Over your flood the life that sought the sunrise faces ours
  that has followed the evening star.

The long migrations meet across you and it is nothing to
  you, you have forgotten us, mother.
You were much younger when we crawled out of the womb
  and lay in the sun's eye on the tideline.

It was long and long ago; we have grown proud since then
  and you have grown bitter; life retains
Your mobile soft unquiet strength; and envies hardness, the
  insolent quietness of stone.

The tides are in our veins, we still mirror the stars, life is
  your child, but there is in me
Older and harder than life and more impartial, the eye that
  watched before there was an ocean.

That watched you fill your beds out of the condensation of
    thin vapor and watched you change them,
That saw you soft and violent wear your boundaries down,
    eat rock, shift places with the continents.

Mother, though my song's measure is like your surf-beat's
    ancient rhythm I never learned it of you.
Before there was any water there were tides of fire, both
    our tones flow from the older fountain.

THE END